THE CONTEMPORARY
BUTTERCREAM BIBLE

THE CONTEMPORARY
BUTTERCREAM BIBLE

Valeri Valeriano & Christina Ong

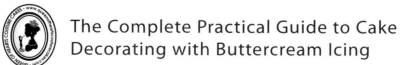

The Complete Practical Guide to Cake
Decorating with Buttercream Icing

D&C
David and Charles

www.stitchcraftcreate.co.uk

CONTENTS

INTRODUCTION

Welcome to the first complete contemporary guide to using buttercream. We are immensely proud to be able to share with you our techniques, tips and ideas – all our expertise – in this book. There is nothing in the world like buttercream. Not only does it allow you to be hugely creative but it also tastes absolutely delicious. It's a winning combination!

We know through our own experience that it takes practice to produce great results, but you will be amazed at the stunning and intricate designs you can achieve straight away with buttercream. Don't be daunted, just dive in and try a few techniques. You don't need a lot of equipment, we didn't start with anything. You don't need to be a brilliant artist, we discovered that working with buttercream unleashed a creative streak we didn't really know we had. You do need a sense of adventure and a willingness to look for inspiration everywhere. Soon you'll be piping pretty cupcakes and beautiful couture cakes. Just remember that not so long ago we were exactly like you...

HUMBLE BEGINNINGS

We just can't help but smile (often a little teary eyed) whenever we share the story of how Queen of Hearts Couture Cakes came about. We could never have imagined that buttercream would bring us to where we are now. It really changed our lives.

Working and living a thousand miles away from your family is hard. Our familes are in the Philippines, however, we are very blessed to have met wonderful friends in the UK who treat us like their family. So on Mother's Day in 2011, we wanted to give our two 'second-moms' something more special than just a card and bouquet of flowers. We decided to bake something for them. And so we scoured the internet (because we didn't have any recipe books) for ideas until we stumbled on a video tutorial on how to make a sunflower cupcake using an improvised piping bag made from a plastic food storage bag. A few more clicks and we watched a tutorial on how to pipe a rose, camellia, chrysanthemum, then a whole cupcake bouquet! We instantly fell in love with the idea and can still remember our excitement to try it.

We didn't have any baking equipment at all, so the following day we went to the supermarket to buy the

ingredients, and then off to the discount store for a silicone cupcake baking tray and spatula, and then we also bought the cheapest hand mixer we could find. Oh yes! We were ready and we didn't waste a single second. Before long a lovely smell filled our tiny house – not just the kitchen but the entire house! There was no room for a full-size oven, so we used to do all our baking in a tiny 5L electric oven, which lived on top of the fridge. Crazy... funny... but it's true.

And so there they were, our first ever half dozen gorgeous golden brown dome-y cupcakes. We had our improvised piping (pastry) bags ready and followed the video tutorial step by step. *Tadaaa!* Our first ever sunflower cupcake. We also attempted to pipe roses and they turned out to be... flowers.

So the special day came and we surprised our friends with our homemade gift. They both really loved it even though some the cupcakes were coming off the wrappers. One of them, Aida, was really the person who convinced us to improve our skills and suggested the idea of making a business out of it. It was as if she saw something in that first, slightly wonky bouquet. She made us feel that there was real potential there. So we kept practising, fell in love with piping until we became obsessed, and that was really the start of it all.

BUILDING OUR BUSINESS

We kept practising, we set up a Facebook page and a website, but no orders arrived for our fledgling business. Meanwhile we kept bombarding Aida with our baking efforts until we finally developed a really good cupcake recipe. Then one day, we had a call from a local school asking if we would be able to join their summer fair. It was in three days time. Without hesitation, we said yes.

Right there and then, we started working on it using just our tiny oven – all we can remember is that we barely slept just to prepare for our first ever fair. Our efforts paid off, we were so overwhelmed with the responses from everyone. When a lady approached us and asked us if we would be interested in taking a pitch at a larger local event, we gave her a hug!

And so we went to another event, and then another, and then another. We had to move to a bigger place as the business got bigger. Not only that, but we also went from cupcakes to bigger cakes and then even bigger wedding cakes. We have literally never stopped since.

We practise and practise and practise whenever we have time, even now. And from local fairs, we are now being invited to big exhibition shows, to teach around the world and to contribute to magazines and blogs. We are also very proud to have been invited to join The Experimental Food Society which is an organization formed to front the UK's most talented and pioneering culinary creatives. It is really quite overwhelming!

INSPIRATION AND INNOVATION

We are often being asked where we get our inspiration from. Our answer is, anything beautiful, from fabrics to paintings, dresses to photos, anything eye-catching that we could translate into an edible form of art. One thing that we would share with you is to keep *innovating*. Don't just settle for what's already there or what everyone else is doing. Dig into your imagination and keep on trying and exploring different ways and techniques.

We hope these things will help you in your cake journey, just like they did for us. So join us as we continuously strive to revive and modernize this age-old Buttercream Art. We hope that we can be an inspiration to all of you who are starting or growing their own cake business, and those who are simply baking at home. If you feel frustrated or you are running out of patience, just think about those two girls that started baking using a small 5L table-top oven and ended up writing *The Contemporary Buttercream Bible*. Just think of them and you will feel much better knowing that if you put your whole heart into whatever you are doing, you will make it!

BUTTERCREAM BASICS

It's really important to learn and eventually master the basics of buttercream because you will find that you use the same simple recipe, techniques and equipment over and over again. Once you understand the nature of buttercream, you will know how to get the very best creative results from it.

MAKING BUTTERCREAM

We strongly believe that our buttercream recipe is at the very heart of this book. It is the most important element that enables us to create amazing couture cakes, as we will show you in the following chapters. Buttercream is a delicate medium, and you do need to understand its characteristics in order to get the most from it.

BASIC BUTTERCREAM RECIPE

With this recipe, the *one* thing you should remember is **never over-beat your buttercream**. If you do it will become grainy and the edges of your petals are likely to 'break' when you pipe flowers. A hand-held mixer is not usually as powerful as a stand mixer, so if you are using a hand-held mixer, make sure you fold your mixture manually first until the ingredients are incorporated. This helps to avoid over-beating as well.

It is a common misunderstanding that to make the buttercream 'light and fluffy' you must beat it for five to ten minutes or even longer. This is true in a way, because if you do this you will incorporate so much air into your buttercream that it will have lots of holes and 'air-pockets', but it will also be grainy and difficult to work with. Don't be tempted to over-beat!

YOU WILL NEED...

- 227g (8oz) butter, room temperature
- 113g (4oz) medium soft vegetable fat (shortening) (Trex), at room temperature, OR 227g (8oz) of soft spreadable vegetable fat (shortening) (Crisco)
- 2-3 tsp vanilla essence, or your choice of flavouring
- 1 tbsp water or milk (omit if you live in a hot country or whenever the temperature is hot)
- 600g (1lb 5oz) icing (confectioners') sugar, sifted, if you are using medium soft vegetable fat (shortening) OR 750g (1lb 10oz) icing sugar, sifted, if you are using soft spreadable vegetable fat (shortening)
- Mixer (hand-held or stand mixer)
- Mixing bowls
- Spatula
- Sieve (sifter/strainer)
- Measuring spoons

ABOUT VEGETABLE FAT, AKA SHORTENING

This is a white solid fat made from vegetable oils, such as soybean and cotton seed oil, and is usually flavourless, bland or neutral in taste. It is ideal for pastry, baking and cake decorating. It plays a very important role in our recipe as it helps make our buttercream stable. It also allows the surface of the decorated cake to 'crust' so that it is not too sticky. And since it makes it stable, you do not need to add too much icing sugar to make a stiff consistency, thus your frosting has just the right sweetness.

There are so many brands of vegetable fat (shortening) and they all have different consistencies. Don't choose one that is too hard as that will not be suitable. The ideal consistency is something soft and spreadable particularly when it's at room temperature. In this particular recipe, vegetable fat (shortening) cannot be substituted with margarine, vegetable oil, ghee or lard as these all have a different colour or melting point, and a very strong taste. See right for a list of popular brands.

TIP

You may substitute vegetable fat (shortening) with powdered milk or coffee creamer. Surprised? It's true! Powdered milk is a dry ingredient and this will make your buttercream stiff and allow it to crust slightly, but it's not as stable as vegetable fat (shortening). Also, it might overpower your flavouring as it can taste too creamy. You may add a little bit of powdered milk to your recipe if you need to stiffen it, but also consider just increasing the amount of icing sugar.

Popular brands of vegetable fat (shortening)

- UK: Trex, Flora White, Cookeen
- USA: Stater Bros, Sweetex, Spectrum, Earth Balance, Crisco
- Ireland: Frytex
- France: St Hubert Pur Végétal
- Italy: Il Grasso Vegetale, Burrolì
- Greece: Nea Fytini
- Cyprus: Spry
- Other Mediterranean countries: Dorina
- Canada: Tenderflake All Vegetable Shortening
- South America: Clover, Doral
- South Africa: Holsum
- Australia: Copha, Solite
- Singapore: Redman
- Malaysia: Krimwel
- India: Olivia, Bake Master
- Most other countries: Crisco

As we have described above, different brands of vegetable fat (shortening) have different consistencies. If the consistency of your shortening is somewhat medium-soft to slightly hard, like Trex, use 113g (4oz) in the recipe below. If it is soft and very spreadable, like Crisco, you will have to double the amount to 227g (8oz).

Also note that these are popular brands around the world, but we have not tried all of them. We recommend you experiment until you find one that works best for you.

1 First rule: If you are beating the butter alone, you may beat it for as long as you want.
Beat butter at medium speed until soft and pale (about one to two minutes). Some brands of butter are more yellow in colour, so to make it paler you can increase the beating time to about two to five minutes (A).

TIP

Don't be tempted to over-beat once the vegetable fat (shortening) has been added, or your buttercream will become grainy and difficult to work with.

A

2 **Second rule: As soon as you add anything to the butter, you must limit your beating time to 20–30 seconds or even less.**
Add the vegetable fat (shortening) and beat for another 20–30 seconds or less. Make sure to read the notes about vegetable fat to determine how much you need to use. Make sure that it is well incorporated and that there are no lumps (B).

3 **Third rule: You may add milk but if you do you can only keep your buttercream for two to four days, as milk has a shorter shelf-life. If you use water, you will be able to keep it for longer – about five to ten days.**
Add vanilla essence, or your flavour of choice (C) and water, or milk (D), then beat at medium speed for about 10–20 seconds until well incorporated.

TIP
Some brands of vegetable fat (shortening) can be very hard, especially when straight from the fridge. You may try allowing it to stand at room temperature for a while, and then, before adding it to your recipe, beat for 30 seconds to a minute.

4 Slowly add the sifted icing (confectioners') sugar and beat at medium speed for another 20–30 seconds or until everything is combined. You may want to fold the ingredients together manually before beating to avoid puffing clouds of sugar round your kitchen (E). Make sure you scrape the sides and bottom of your bowl, as well as the blade of your mixer, so you don't miss any lumps of icing sugar.

5 Lastly, after scraping the bowl, beat again for about 20–30 seconds and **do not over-mix**. This yields a perfect piping consistency of buttercream frosting (F).

TIP

What is so good about our recipe is that a little less or more of a certain ingredient is fine. So if your buttercream is too stiff, add water or milk. If it is too thin, just add icing (confectioners') sugar. Adjust it as you need to – all in moderation of course. You may use your buttercream straight away to cover and decorate your cakes but we suggest you chill it in the fridge for about an hour for best results.

COVERAGE

If you make the basic buttercream recipe with the amounts given, one batch will yield about approximately 1–1.1kg (2lb 7½oz) of buttercream. This will be enough to cover the top, the sides and fill a 20cm (8in) round or square cake, or decorate about 20–30 cupcakes, depending on the design. This can be your guide to determine how much frosting you need to prepare. If you have any left over, just label it with the date you made it and store it in the fridge.

STABLE VERSUS UNSTABLE

We say buttercream is stable if it can hold its shape, regardless of the warmth of climate. Unstable buttercream of course is not like this. Trying to work with unstable buttercream is the most common problem we see, so we came up with a really stable recipe that does not sacrifice the yumminess of the buttercream.

The photo on the right illustrates both consistencies. When buttercream is stable (right), you will see that the edges of the swirl are very precise and it holds its shape well. On the other hand, the unstable swirl on the left looks droopy and soft and just doesn't hold its shape well at all.

TIP

Keep your buttercream inside the refrigerator (chiller) and store it in an air-tight container or food storage bags. You can freeze it for up to a month, letting it defrost thoroughly at room temperature before use. Do not beat it again in a mixer, just mix it manually. But of course, nothing is better than fresh buttercream!

ADDING FLAVOURS

The flavour of the buttercream will enhance the character of your cake. Your choice may be influenced by the occasion, your own taste or that of the recipients, or even by different cultures. Buttercream is flavour-friendly – you can easily play with flavourings, adding just a hint or making them as strong as you wish.

There are lots of different flavours you can add to your buttercream. They come in the form of powder, liquid (essence/extracts/oils/liqueurs) and paste, or can include cream, jam, fruits, melted chocolates, tea bags, and so many other ingredients. You may or may not choose to omit the vanilla essence before adding the flavour of your choice. To simplify things, when adding any of these flavourings to your buttercream, just be mindful of the consistency. You do not have to adjust the amount of icing sugar or butter initially, just make a batch of buttercream according to our recipe, then add your flavouring. If it becomes too soft at this stage, add a little bit of icing sugar, or if it becomes too stiff, add a little bit of water. Simple.

Be cautious when adding squashed or pureed fruits as these have a high water content that may change your buttercream consistency dramatically.

Strawberry jam

Peanut butter

Coffee

Vanilla extract

Crushed Oreo cookies

Squashed blueberries

Cocoa powder

Melted chocolate

Green tea

EQUIPMENT

In the following chapters we will be using plenty of tools and equipment, in a wide range of sizes and shapes – some commonplace, others more unusual. You will find out all about the use of each one as we discuss the different decorating techniques. Everything listed below can be easily sourced from a local specialist baking shop or online suppliers.

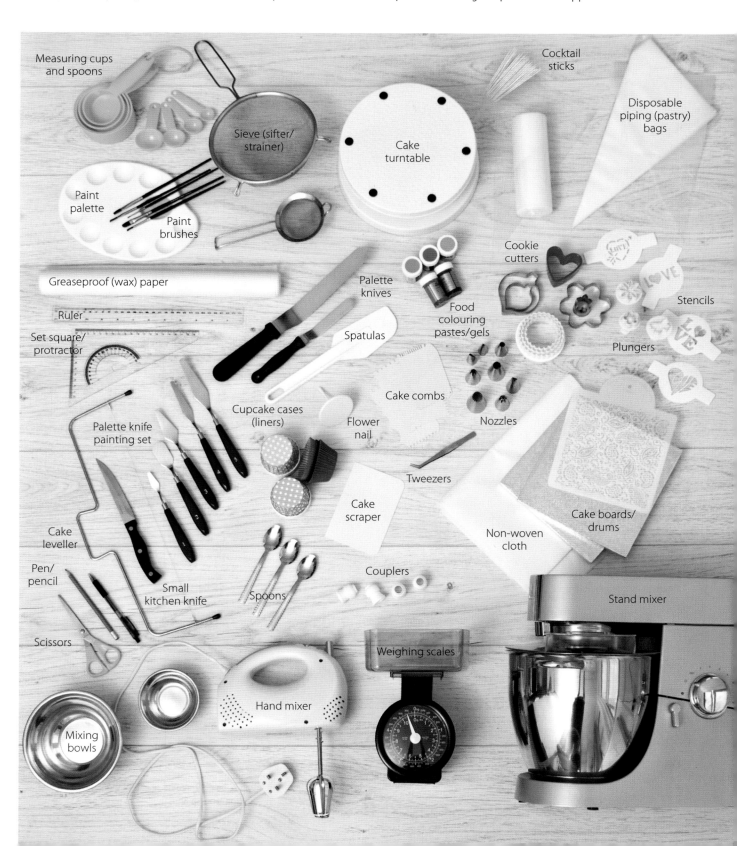

Measuring cups and spoons

Cocktail sticks

Disposable piping (pastry) bags

Sieve (sifter/strainer)

Cake turntable

Paint palette

Paint brushes

Greaseproof (wax) paper

Palette knives

Cookie cutters

Stencils

Ruler

Food colouring pastes/gels

Set square/protractor

Spatulas

Plungers

Cake combs

Palette knife painting set

Cupcake cases (liners)

Flower nail

Nozzles

Tweezers

Cake boards/drums

Cake scraper

Non-woven cloth

Cake leveller

Pen/pencil

Couplers

Stand mixer

Small kitchen knife

Spoons

Scissors

Weighing scales

Mixing bowls

Hand mixer

NOZZLE GUIDE

Piping nozzles (also called piping tips) are those plastic or stainless steel points that fit on the end of a piping (pastry) bag and that the frosting is forced through to create different effects. They come in different sizes and brands, and each brand has their corresponding numbers or letters inscribed on them to indicate the output.

Here, we have illustrated all the different nozzles we have used in this book. Each nozzle will produce a different effect. For best results, the piping bag and its nozzle have to be held at the correct angle as well, and we will teach you all about that that as we discuss piping techniques in the following chapters.

Big round   Large round peak   Simple round swirl   Dots

Writing   Writing   Lace   Brushed embroidery   Zigzag   Crochet

Petal   Hydrangea   Camellia   Rose   Daisy   Ruffles

Leaf   Leaves   Leaf texture   Sunflower   Blades of grass/foliage

Chrysanthemum

Chrysanthemum

Border

Reversed border

Basketweave

Traditional
basketweave

Queen of Hearts
basketweave

Closed star

Closed star peak

Rosette/closed star swirl

c-motion (top)
e-motion (bottom)

Fleur-de-lis

Open star

Open star peak

Star swirl

BAGS AND NOZZLES TERMINOLOGY

Piping nozzles are also known as 'tips' in various parts of the world, but for brevity we will just refer to them as nozzles from this point forwards in this book. In the same way, piping bags are sometimes called 'pastry bags', but in order not to be too 'word-y' we'll just call them piping bags from here on in.

French

French peak

French swirl

COLOURING BUTTERCREAM

The colours you use will bring your cake to life. Choosing the right colour combination
is essential to make the design more natural, or more striking. In this section we will tell
you how to blend these colours without sacrificing the quality of your buttercream.

This colour wheel, basically a rainbow in a circle, is a great way to see how colours relate to one another. Adjacent colours, for
example blue and green, will always have a pleasing harmony, but colours that are directly opposite one another on the wheel,
for example green and red, will also create a lovely vibrant combination. Experiment until you find colours that you love.

To tint your buttercream you can use food colouring pastes or gels, and the amount you add will determine the vibrancy of your colour. Pastes and gels blend well with the buttercream and the colours do not bleed. We do not recommend using food colouring powders and liquids, as both can affect the consistency of your frosting and will create a high tendency for the colours to bleed. Liquid colours will make your frosting soft, and if you use powder, you will find that after about 24 hours some of the tiny particles that did not totally dissolve on mixing will create blotches of colour. In addition, the powders sometimes have either a salty or bitter taste.

To regulate the amount of colouring you add, we recommend that you use a cocktail stick (toothpick), dipping it into your colour then adding it to the buttercream in tiny amounts at a time until you get your desired shade. Do not re-use the cocktail stick after it has touched the buttercream or it will contaminate the colouring and could make it go off.

A RULE WHEN ADDING COLOUR

Remember our 'golden rule' when making your buttercream and **do not over-beat.** Bear in mind that when you mix in the food colouring, that counts as additional beating. To minimize this, smear the food colouring into the buttercream with a spatula or the back of a spoon first until you see that there are no more lumps or blobs of gel or paste then fold-smear-fold-smear-fold your buttercream until you get an even colour.

MIXING COLOURS

To tint your buttercream to make pastel and light colours is easy. Bright and deep colours like navy blue, black and red are the hardest colours to achieve. But bear in mind as well that buttercream tends to become a shade darker after while. Let the information below help you when tinting your frosting.

TIP

If you ever need to cover and decorate a big cake and you want to be very particular about the colour, it is better to prepare too much buttercream than too little as it will be hard to mix the same colour again.

Navy blue

To get a rich navy blue colour, we usually combine few shades of blue like Sugarflair Baby Blue, and Navy Blue (but not Sugarflair Ice Blue, which is too light and bright) and a small amount of brown or black food colouring paste or gel.

Black

To tint your buttercream to a true black, we suggest adding sifted cocoa powder (unsweetened cocoa) to your buttercream until it becomes dark brown then add black food colouring paste or gel. Cocoa is a dry ingredient so it will make your buttercream a little stiff so add few drops of water to adjust its consistency. The amount of cocoa you use will depend on how deep a shade you wish to make.

Red

To make your buttercream bright red, combine even amounts of any dark shade of pink (Sugarflair Claret or Dusky Pink), plus orange (Sugarflair Orange or Tangerine) and any shade of red (Sugarflair Ruby or Poppy Red). To make a really deep red, add a hint of black or brown food colouring paste or gel.

FILLING THE PIPING BAG

We find that the easiest, least messy and most effective way of filling a piping bag is by using a tall glass or vase to hold the bag and then using a spoon or a spatula to scoop the buttercream in. Try it and we think you'll agree.

If you are using a nozzle, remember to fit this in the tip of the bag before filling it with buttercream by cutting a hole for the nozzle to poke through, just large enough for about half of its length to protude out of the bag. Start with a small hole and make it bigger if necessary, because if you cut too large a hole straight off, your bag will be ruined. Do not be tempted to overfill the bag, as you will end up in a sticky mess! When the bag is sufficiently full twist the top firmly to secure.

ATTACHING A COUPLER

Sometimes we use a tool called a coupler (see Equipment). This two-part device lets you interchange several nozzles without changing the bag. The two parts of the coupler are called the base (the bigger part) and the ring. You basically cut the tip off your piping bag to leave just enough of an opening, put the base inside the bag (narrow end first), put the nozzle of your choice over the portion of the base that sticks out of the bag then screw the ring on to lock the nozzle on. A coupler also secures your nozzle from popping out if the piping bag tears (which can sometimes happen if you use low-quality bags or squeeze too strongly!).

TIP

Some designs will require you to fill a piping bag with more than one colour of buttercream. In this case it is best to put each colour into a separate piping bag and then pipe them into a new bag (see Up and Down Two-Tone Ruffles, Piping Textures and Patterns).

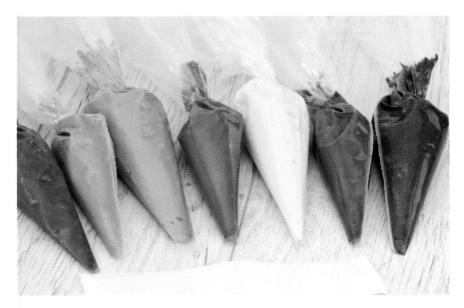

INSPIRATIONS

We are always asked, 'Your cakes are all unique — where do you get your inspiration from?' Our secret is simple. We get inspiration from anything beautiful and interesting, from absolutely everywhere! Look around you, and if a certain colour or design catches your eye the next thing you should do is imagine how you will put it on your cake.

COVERING CAKES

Here we will discuss how to cover your cake properly, making sure that the buttercream sticks to the cake and provides a clean base for any additional decoration. Buttercream is physically heavy and if you don't learn to cover correctly, then the buttercream might fall off the cake. The first essential stage is crumb coating, so we'll begin there.

CRUMB COATING

As the name suggests, this is all about coating the crumbs! This technique means applying a thin layer of buttercream around your cake to secure the loose crumbs, before adding the decorative layers and features. This is a very important step that you should not miss, as this makes your outer layer of buttercream stick to the cake, giving the heavy piped and textured designs something to adhere to.

A

B

1 You can use a palette knife to apply the buttercream to the cake, but some cake sponges can be very crumbly. When you use a palette knife, the tendency is to keep pushing and pressing the frosting and this might damage your cake. Instead, we use a piping bag to apply the frosting (A).

2 Use a round nozzle or just snip the end off a piping bag. Using the same frosting that will go on the rest of the cake, fill the piping bag and pipe around the cake with a good pressure so it sticks to the cake (B).

3 Use your palette knife to spread the buttercream, using even pressure (C).

4 Next you can use a cake scraper to level out the thickness of the frosting and to remove any excess (D).

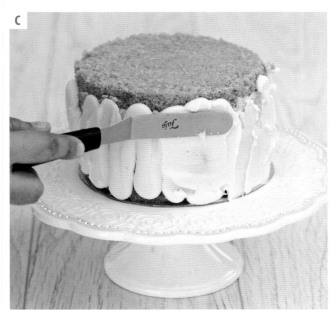

C

D

TIP
It is best to put the cake in the fridge after you have crumb coated it, for about 30 minutes to an hour (or quick freeze it for 10–15 minutes) or until the surface is hard enough to work on before you apply any more buttercream decoration.

SMOOTHING

After the cake has been chilled for a short while you can apply another layer of buttercream and create a smooth surface. The thickness of this layer will be a matter of taste. To be able to perfectly smooth a cake takes patience and practice. Trust us, you will not be able to 'perfectly perfect' it on your first go, but after a while you will get so practised at it that it will become easy.

PALETTE KNIFE

This is the common way of smoothing a cake – no fancy tool, just a palette knife. You simply have to spread the buttercream frosting around the cake using the knife. The finish though is not perfectly smooth as the knife will leave few lines and ridges.

You can use any palette knife, straight or cranked, and the best choice of size will depend on the size of your cake. We find it is best to use a short crank-handled knife for most occasions. The direction in which you spread doesn't matter, but it is important to remove any excess and to make an even layer.

TIP
Applying a buttercream layer with a palette knife will allow you to create an artistic finish. Don't expect the surface to be perfectly smooth with this method.

CAKE SCRAPER

Make sure that the edge of your scraper is perfectly smooth. Remember that any dent on your scraper will be visible on your cake because buttercream is soft and delicate. Using a plain edge scraper is a fairly quick way of smoothing your cake. With the cake on a turntable, hold the scraper upright and perpendicular to the work surface, and run it around your cake until smooth.

If your cake is tall you may need to use a longer implement, such as a ruler, a big cake lifter or (the most effective tool we've found) an L ruler or 90 degree triangle ruler.

TIP
For best results we highly recommend that you place your cake on a thin cake board that is about 0.5–1cm (¼–½in) larger than the cake. See photograph B opposite. As you run your cake scraper around you can press against the edge of the board, rather than on the cake side, ensuring an even layer of buttercream and preventing you from pressing too hard on the cake.

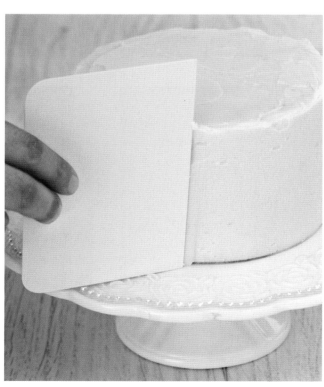

NON-WOVEN CLOTH

The following technique is similar to the 'Viva paper towel method' that is being used to smooth buttercream covered cakes in the USA. However, if you don't live in the States, you will need an alternative that you can source locally, so we have spent some time researching a product that can be found all over the world. We tried and tried different mediums until we came up with using a non-woven cloth, which has a smooth side and does not stick to the buttercream. Non-woven cloth may come in plain white or with minimal design. A good example of this is the interfacing fabric that is used in sewing. You can buy this by the metre or yard and it is very cheap. You can use any other similar non-woven fabric as long as it is really smooth and has no holes or ridges.

1 Make sure that you use either a palette knife or a scraper to smooth and get rid of most of the lines or ridges in the buttercream before the surface crusts. This will be very helpful later during the actual smoothing process.

2 Since our buttercream recipe is a 'crusting' type of frosting, it is important that you wait until the surface is dry to the touch, usually 10–20 minutes. Test this by gently touching the surface (A). If it still sticks on your finger, it means you have to let it stand for few more minutes at room temperature. Don't chill it in the fridge as this is a moist environment and will obviously not help in drying.

3 Using the smooth side of your non-woven cloth, place it onto the surface of the cake and rub the cloth using your fingers to flatten any ridges and unevenness (B).

4 Slowly peel the cloth away and check if there are still parts that need smoothing. Instead of rubbing again, use a plain edge cake scraper gently and with a little bit of pressure (C), running it over the cloth and all the away around the cake until perfectly smooth (D).

TIP
When smoothing the side of the cake we usually start from the bottom and work upwards. We then scrape horizontally all around the cake before smoothing from the bottom up again until we get a perfectly smooth finish.

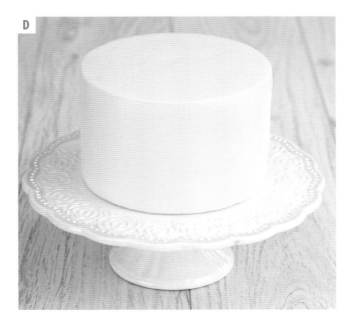

SHARP EDGES

A couple of wise men and women of the cake decorating industry once told us that if you want to create sharp edges on your cake, they must be absolutely flawless. This can be a little tricky to achieve in the beginning, but as we always say, practice is the only secret.

It is very important to remove any excess buttercream to achieve sharp edges, otherwise you will find yourself in an endless repetitive loop: smooth the side, excess goes to the top, smooth the top, excess goes to the side *ad infinitum*!

1 Using a palette knife, scraper or a small kitchen knife, trim the bumpy excess buttercream around the edge of the cake. (A)

2 Apply the non-woven cloth on the surface and smooth again with a help of a cake scraper (B).

TIP
Fresh buttercream gets exposed when you trim the edges, so wait for it to crust again before applying the non-woven cloth.

BEFORE YOU DECORATE...

Let's make it clear that the steps for covering your cake with a smooth finish are as follows:

1. Crumb coat
2. Apply a layer of buttercream and level/smooth with a palette knife
3. Smooth with a cake scraper
4. Smooth further with non-woven cloth
5. Create sharp edges

Important! In the chapters that follow we have created at least one couture cake to demonstrate the technique we have shown in that chapter. It is assumed in the instruction for creating the cake that you have already crumb coated it. Note that you will need about 200–300g (7–10½oz) of plain buttercream to crumb coat each cake. This quantity is not included in the requirements list for the cake.

TEXTURED FINISH

Rather than making the surface perfectly smooth, here is another way of covering your cake.
The results can be achieved in a flash just by using some simple tools.

Fork
Simply run the fork over the surface of your cake in whichever direction you wish. You can even do a wavy motion.

Palette knife
By using a simple palette knife, you can give another textured finish on your cake. Different stokes will result in various lovely effects.

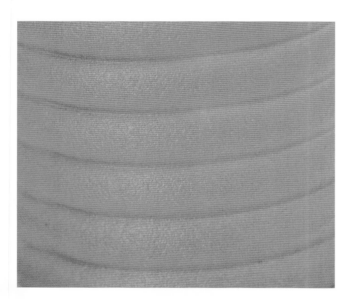

Cake comb
Cake combs are another fantastic tool for creating texture. They are made of either thin plastic or metal and have different contoured edges – waves, ridges and swirls. You just run the edge of the scraper around your cake to form ridges. To get the best result, comb your cake when the buttercream is freshly applied and use a cake turntable.

Impression mats
Impression mats (also called texture mats) are plastic or silicone sheets with fantastic designs that will allow you to emboss prints directly into the surface of your cake. They are mostly used for sugarpaste (rolled fondant) but since our buttercream recipe is a 'crusting' type, you will be able to use these sheets. Just make sure that surface of the cake has already crusted properly by touching it gently with your finger.

COVERING BOARDS

Since our method of cake decorating is is all about buttercream, you might guess that we do not use any other medium. However, it is tricky to cover your board with buttercream so we have thought of a more creative way of doing it.

In everything we do, we try to make the technique easy, be adventurous and create brilliant results. So if we are using a cake board, we always choose the most exciting materials we can source, like fancy papers, fabrics, and colourful tissue papers. To these you can add on accessories that will complement the design of the cake. Make sure you don't over do it – avoid colours that clash with your cake design, and make sure nothing upstages your cake, which should, after all, be the centre of attention.

YOU WILL NEED...

- Ribbons, buttons, ruffles, lace
- Wrapping paper, colourful tissue paper, crêpe paper, fabrics
- Glue gun/stick (hot melt), double sided tape, clear tape, adhesive spray, craft glue
- Scissors
- Pen or pencil
- Clear cellophane, contact paper/sheet

TIP
You may come across all sorts of different shapes of board – hearts, ovals and hexagons. Follow the advice for covering a square board for all the angular shapes, and the instructions for a round board for the curvy ones.

SQUARE
Whatever the size of cake board you are covering, cut your chosen paper or fabric about 5–7.5cm (2–3in) and your cellophane or contact paper about 13–15cm (5–6in) larger all round than the board, then cut across the corners as shown. Place your paper on the board and fold all the sides under, then secure on the back of the board with clear tape. Make sure that the paper does not have any lint, icing or any debris stuck to it, then repeat the same process with your cellophane or contact paper to cover it. Put matching ribbons or buttons or anything else you have chosen around the edge your board.

ROUND
Covering a circular board is basically the same as covering a square. Follow the instructions above, but instead of snipping the corners, you just have to make small cuts approximately 2cm (1in) apart and up to the board all the way around your paper before you secure each piece with clear tape. Repeat with the cellophane or contact paper, then finish with accessories around the board.

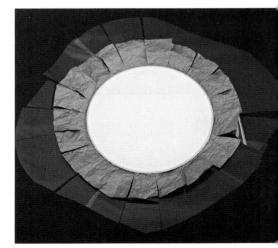

DOWELLING

Anything that is complex and made up of different parts will need some structure to hold everything together in one piece. The same principle applies to stacking layers of cake. You will need plastic or wooden dowels, inserted properly into the lower tiers of a cake, to bear the weight of the layers above and to make sure that each cake layer does not get squashed and collapse.

YOU WILL NEED...

- Dowel rods, plastic or wooden
- Wire cutter, big scissors or serrated knife
- Pen or pencil
- Thin cake board
- Ruler
- Cocktail stick (toothpick)

TIP
Instructions for making the cake opposite can be found in the Lace tutorial, in the Textiles Effects chapter.

1 Measure the height of the bottom tier of your cake with a ruler. This measurement will be the guide for cutting your dowel rods. Use wire cutters, big scissors or a serrated knife to carefully cut as many dowels as you need (see step three) to the same length (A).

TIP
To measure the height of your cake tier you can push a dowel right into it from the top until it touches the cake board, then mark the place on the dowel that the cake frosting reaches, using a pencil or pen, then remove the dowel and cut it off at the marked length.

2 On a piece of paper or a thin cardboard, mark out the outline of the next tier up and cut the paper or card to size. Centre this template on the bottom tier of the cake and use a cocktail stick (toothpick) to clearly mark the outline (B).

3 Mark the position for the dowels and insert the dowel rods into the bottom tier, evenly spaced about 4cm (1½in) in from the edge of the marked outline (C). Push the dowel rods straight down until each touches the cake board (D). The number of dowels to put into the cake depends on the size of the cake. The bigger the cake, the more dowels required.

4 Repeat this procedure for every tier on the cake. If it is really a tall cake, you will need to insert a long dowel straight through all the tiers, through the centre of the cake to stabilize it.

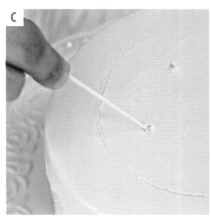

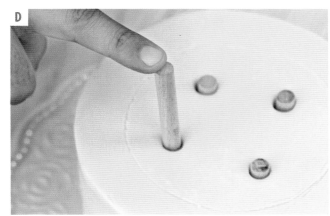

CUPCAKES

Cupcakes are always fun to bake – there's less pressure than when you make a full-size cake. You can try out swirls and peaks and perfect your piping technique with these basic patterns. However, the small scale of a cupcake also allows you to practise the piped flowers you will find in the following chapters. Why not try one of each flowers to create a lovely garden of buttercream? Then check out how to make a cupcake bouquet at the end of the Piping Flowers chapter.

As well as ideas for a range of lovely patterns and textures to pipe on your cupcakes, on the following pages we will also share a simple adaptable cupcake recipe that always works for us.

SIMPLE CUPCAKE RECIPE

This is a great basic recipe, which you can adapt to suit your needs by swapping the vanilla extract for a variety of other flavourings.

YOU WILL NEED...

- 150g (5½oz) plain flour
- 150g (5½oz) sugar
- 150g (5½oz) butter
- 2 eggs
- 2 tbsp milk
- ¼ tsp baking powder
- ½ tsp salt
- 1-2 tsp pure vanilla extract
- Mixer (hand-held or stand mixer)
- Mixing bowls
- Spatula
- Sieve (sifter/strainer)
- Measuring spoons
- Two twelve-hole cupcake baking pans
- Cupcake cases (liners)
- Oven thermometer (optional)

Makes about 15–18 standard size cupcakes.

1 Preheat the oven to 150°C/300°F/Gas Mark 2. If the temperature is too high, there is a tendency for your cupcakes to rise too much and become 'domed'.

2 Using a mixer, beat together the butter and sugar in a bowl for about 20–30 seconds, or until light and fluffy. Add the eggs, vanilla extract and milk to the bowl and beat for another 10–20 seconds, or until the mixture is smooth.

3 In another bowl, sift together the flour, baking powder and salt, and set aside.

4 Combine the wet and dry ingredients. Reduce the mixer speed to low-medium and beat for 20–40 seconds until all ingredients are just combined, **do not over-beat.** Scrape down the side of the bowl with a spatula.

5 Put one cupcake case in each hole of the cupcake baking pans. You won't have enough batter for all 24 holes, probably nearer 15 or 18.

6 Divide the batter between the paper cases and fill cases about two thirds full. We use an ice cream scoop to distribute the batter equally. It is best to use greaseproof (wax paper) cupcake or muffin cases as the plain paper ones have a tendency to peel off the cakes.

7 Bake in the middle of the oven until the cupcakes have risen and are just firm to the touch in the centre. Check your cupcakes after 20–22 minutes by inserting a cocktail stick (toothpick). If it comes out clean, the cupcakes are ready. Remove them carefully from the pan and let them cool on a wire rack.

TIP

The temperature inside your oven plays a major role in achieving perfectly baked goodies. To avoid too much rising or sinking of your cakes you need the temperature to be a constant 150–160°C (300–325°F/Gas mark 2–3). Therefore we highly recommend using an oven thermometer. Keep one handy so that you can be sure you have the right temperature inside your oven.

PIPED PEAKS

This is one of the easiest and cutest ways to decorate a cupcake. All you need is a simple star or round nozzle and a piping bag. Want to make it even simpler? Just get a piping bag and snip off the end to make a little hole the same size as a simple round nozzle.

1 You can either use a big star or a round nozzle to create these peaks. In this demonstration we have used a star nozzle and the two-tone technique described in the Piping Textures and Ruffles chapter. Hold your piping bag at a 45 degree angle with your nozzle slightly above the surface of the cupcake (A).

2 Squeeze piping bag until the buttercream comes out and forms a blob then slowly pull away your nozzle. When you have reached the height that you wish, stop squeezing your piping bag and pull away abruptly to form a nice peak (B).

3 Repeat the process (C) until the cupcake is fully covered. You can pipe peaks on top of each other for a more towering effect.

If you are using a star nozzle, it is nice to twist nozzle while pulling the piping bag away.

This cupcake was decorated using a plain round nozzle to make smooth peaks.

PIPED SWIRLS

Swirls are another extremely easy way to decorate cupcakes. As long as you have a piping bag and a star or plain nozzle, you are ready to pipe away! Colour and flavour the buttercream or decorate it with sprinkles of your choice to compliment the flavour of the cupcake and the colour scheme. You can achieve different effects with each style of nozzle.

1 To do the swirls, you can either start from the middle or at the edge of the cupcake.

2 Hold your piping bag at a 45 degree angle with your nozzle slightly above the surface of the cupcake.

3 Give your piping bag a good squeeze until the buttercream comes out and forms a star (A).

4 Without releasing pressure, slowly turn your piping bag in a big spiral motion (B) until the cupcake is covered with buttercream (C).

This swirl is piped with a French star nozzle in the same way as described above, but with the piping bag and nozzle held vertically above the cupcake.

Open star nozzle (Wilton 1M)

Closed star nozzle (Wilton 2D)

French nozzle

Simple round nozzle

PIPING TEXTURES AND PATTERNS

Piping buttercream is the essential skill to learn if you want to use this delicious decorating medium on your cakes. Strangely it's often mistakenly thought to be difficult, but this couldn't be further from the truth. In this chapter we'll show you how to create amazing effects, from ruffles to basketweave, using some really easy techniques, all achieved with a humble piping bag and a handful of nozzles.

RUFFLES

Ruffles are such an easy and effective technique for creating elegant cakes and can be achieved using various different piping motions – back and forth, up and down and zigzag. All can be done quickly and each will create a slightly different effect. In the Back and Forth Ruffles project, we've given the technique a little twist with zigzag panels of ruffles and ombre shading. You'll see how to create a striped two-tone effect in the Up and Down Ruffles tutorial, and how a wiggle plus a squeeze makes a squiggle in the Squiggly Ruffles tutorial.

BACK AND FORTH RUFFLES

1 Cover your cake with thin layer of buttercream, as described in the Buttercream Basics chapter. The surface does not necessarily have to be smooth, as it will be covered by the ruffles (A).

2 Using a side scraper or ruler, measure and mark equal sized narrow triangles around the surface of the cake (B). If you are using alternate colours for your ruffles, make sure you divide the cake into an equal rather than odd number of triangles.

3 Place your chosen colour of buttercream in a piping bag with small petal nozzle (Wilton 104). Begin at the bottom and hold the piping bag vertically with the wide part of the nozzle against the cake. Continuously squeeze the bag in an ascending and back and forth motion, filling the marked triangles (C).

TIP
This type of ruffle uses a lot of buttercream and is therefore heavy, so make sure that each ruffle starts at the very base of the cake so that the weight of the ruffle is supported.

4 As you work your way up the cake, change piping bag to the next shade of buttercream to achieve the gradient effect (D). Make sure you follow the marks on the cake and keep the pressure constant to avoid wavy ruffles.

5 Change piping bag to the next shade of buttercream and continue working up to the top of the cake making your ruffles smaller and smaller as you reach the tip of the triangle (E).

6 Change piping bag and start the next panel of ruffles, this time starting with the smallest ruffles at the base of the cake and working upwards increasing the width following the marks on the cake. For contrast with the gradient ruffles we have used uncoloured buttercream here (F).

7 Continue working around the cake piping the coloured and uncoloured ruffles alternately until you have covered the whole cake. Finish the cake with tiers with different textured finishes as desired.

TO CREATE THIS CAKE...

- 20 x 15cm (8 x 6in) round cake (bottom tier), 15 x 7.5cm (6 x 3in) round cake (middle tier), 13 x 7.5cm (5 x 3in) round cake (top tier)
- Dowel rods
- 800g–1.25kg (1lb 12oz–2lb 12oz) buttercream
- Paste colour: blue (Sugarflair Baby Blue)
- Piping bags
- Small petal nozzle (Wilton 104)
- Cake scraper or ruler
- Palette knife
- Cake stand or covered cake board

Cover, dowel and stack the cakes (see Covering Cakes, Buttercream Basics) and place on a stand or covered board. Cover the top tiers using patting strokes described in the section on palette knife brushstrokes (see Palette Knife Techniques). Leave 200–250g (7–9oz) of buttercream uncoloured, then divide the rest into three portions, colouring each a darker shade of blue. Pipe the ruffles as described in the tutorial and finish by piping ruffle flowers, using the carnation tutorial as a guide, around the middle tier (see Carnation and Sweet Pea, Piping Flowers).

UP AND DOWN TWO-TONE RUFFLES

1 To achieve two-tone ruffles, prepare the colours you have chosen in two separate bags, without any nozzles. Prepare another piping bag with a small petal nozzle (Wilton 104) (A).

2 Cut the ends off the piping bags with the tinted buttercream and squeeze into the bag with the nozzle. The top colour (stripe colour) should be squeezed to the side of the piping bag where the narrow/pointed part of the nozzle is, then squeeze the other colour on top of the first (B). Use the same technique for the other colours.

3 You can now start piping either at the top or the bottom of the cake. Make sure that the narrow/pointed part of the nozzle is pointing in the same direction that you want your ruffles to fall (either up as in C or down as in D).

4 Holding the bag sideways at an angle and with the wide part of the nozzle touching the surface of the cake, continuously squeeze the piping bag with constant pressure and drag it around the cake until the two ends meet. Slightly wiggle your piping bag as you pipe to make wavy ruffles.

5 Repeat the process for the succeeding ruffles making sure that they are close to each other and maintaining the angle (E).

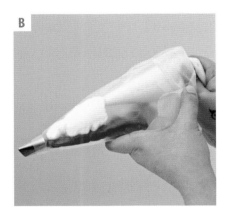

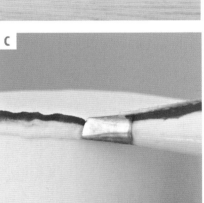

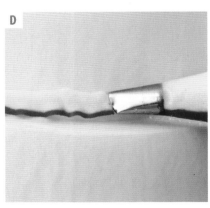

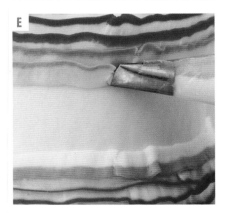

TO CREATE THIS CAKE...

- 20 x 7.5cm (8 x 3in) round cake (bottom tier), 15 x 15cm (6 x 6in) round cake (top tier)
- Dowel rods
- 650g–930g (1lb 7oz–2lb 1oz) buttercream
- Paste colours: red (Sugarflair Ruby Red), orange (Sugarflair Tangerine), yellow (Sugarflair Melon), brown (Sugarflair Dark Brown), dark brown (Sugarflair Dark Brown and Black)
- Small petal nozzle (Wilton 104)
- Piping bags
- Cake stand or covered cake board

Cover the cakes with a smooth finish, dowel and stack the cakes (see Covering Cakes, Buttercream Basics) and place on a stand or covered board. Colour 200–250g (7–9oz) buttercream brown and 50–80g (1¾–3oz) darker brown then cover the bottom tier using a blending effect (see Blending, Palette Knife Techniques) and completing it with a perfectly smooth finish (see Smoothing, Buttercream Basics). Colour 100–150g (3½–5½oz) of buttercream each of red, dark orange, light orange (use a little less Tangerine paste to achieve this) and yellow. Use this and the remaining uncoloured buttercream to pipe the top tier as described in the tutorial, and finish by piping a camelia at the base of the top tier (see, Camellia and Hydrangea, Piping Flowers).

TIP

Make sure you apply slight pressure to the nozzle against the cake to ensure that the ruffles stick to the cake. To adjust the thickness of the 'stripe' just turn your piping nozzle and squeeze the piping bag until you get the desired effect.

SQUIGGLY RUFFLES

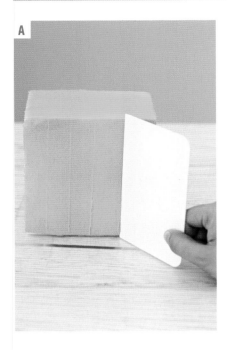

1 Divide and mark the surface of the cake into equal size panels. You can use a ruler, toothpick or side scraper to do this (A).

2 Fit the piping bag with a small petal tip (Wilton 103) and fill with buttercream in your chosen colour (B).

3 Place the wide part of the nozzle against the surface of the cake, then continuously squeeze the piping bag with constant pressure and wiggle slightly in random directions all the way to the top and until you fill each panel (C).

4 Repeat the process on alternate panels, following the marks on the cake (D). In this project, we airbrushed the ruffles with iridescent gold – this is entirely optional but gives a lovely sparkling finish.

TO CREATE THIS CAKE...

- 10 x 7.5cm (4 x 3in) square cake (top tier), 15 x 10cm (6 x 4in) square cake (bottom tier)
- 500–700g (1lb 2oz–1lb 9oz) buttercream
- Dowel rods
- Paste colours: dark purple (Sugarflair Grape Vine) and yellow (mix of Sugarflair Melon and Autumn Leaf)
- Small petal nozzle (Wilton 103)
- Piping bags
- Cake stand or covered cake board
- Airbrush with gold edible paint (optional)

Cover the cakes with a 200–300g (7–10½oz) of yellow buttercream and give them a smooth finish (see Covering Cakes, Butercream Basics), dowel and stack the cakes (see Buttercream Basics) and place on a stand or covered board. Colour 300–400g (10½–14oz) of buttercream purple. Pipe the ruffles as described in the tutorial and pipe a carnation in the centre of each side of the top tier cake (see Carnation and Sweet Pea, Piping Flowers). Finish by airbrushing with gold (optional).

TIP
Make sure you apply sufficient pressure that the ruffles stick to the cake. Buttercream is heavy and you do not want it to fall off the cake!

BASKETWEAVE

Here we simply pipe diagonal lines on to the surface of the cake. The lines will appear to interlace with one another to create a basketweave pattern. First we will show you our very own variation of this technique, which is really easy to achieve and brings the traditional version bang up to date with a contemporary look. Pipe matching flowers on top and your cake will surely take someone's breath away.

1 Measure the height of your cake and divide horizontally to make equal bands of, give or take, 2.5cm (1in). Mark visible guide lines in the crumb coating (A).

2 Before the crumb coat has crusted (so that the weaves will adhere to it), and with the smooth side of the basketweave nozzle (Wilton 48 or 45) pointing upwards, pipe diagonal lines from the bottom of the cake up to the guide line. Use sufficient pressure so the weaves will adhere to the cake properly. Continue piping all the way around the cake (B).

3 Repeat the process and pipe diagonal lines going in the opposite direction for the second layer, and so on. Make sure that there are no gaps and that all 'weaves' are connected (C).

4 For a neat finish at the base, using a darker shade of Mocha tinted buttercream, cut the tip off the piping bag and pipe a thicker border at the bottom using the crochet technique (see Textile Effects chapter) (D).

TIP

It's a nice idea to use gradient shades of brown to resemble a real basket or give a vintage look. You could also use a big chrysanthemum nozzle for a nice variation.

TO CREATE THIS CAKE...

- 15 x 15cm (6 x 6in) square cake
- 1.05–1.4kg (2lb 6oz–3lb 1½oz) buttercream
- Paste colours: light and dark mocha (Sugarflair Mocha), light peach (Sugarflair Peach), pink (Sugarflair Pink), dark green (Sugarflair Spruce Green), light green (Sugarflair Bittermelon)
- Piping bags
- Basketweave nozzle (Wilton 48) or plain basketweave nozzle (Wilton 45)
- Side scraper or ruler
- Cake stand or covered cake board

Cover the cake (see Covering Cakes, Buttercream Basics) and place on a stand or covered board. Colour 400–500g (14oz–1lb 2oz) of buttercream light mocha, and 100–150g (3½–5½oz) a darker shade of mocha. Pipe the basketweave pattern and bottom border as described in the tutorial. Colour the remaining buttercream in the following quantities: 150–200g (5½–7oz) light peach for the roses, 150–200g (5½–7oz) pink for the chrysanthemums, 100–150g (3½–5½oz) dark green for the leaves and 150–200g (5½–7oz) light green for the foliage. Finish by piping roses, chrysanthemums and leaves on top (see Rose and Rosebud, Chrysanthemum and Daffodil, and Sunflower and Leaves, Piping Flowers) and adding light green foliage (see Ruffles, Piping Texture and Patterns) on the top and sides.

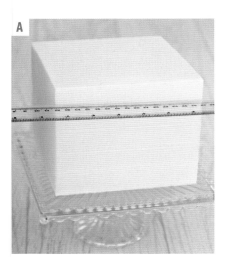

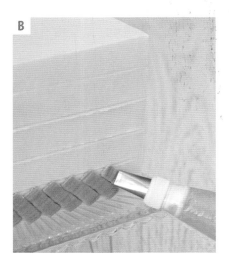

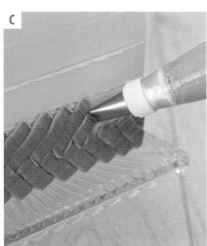

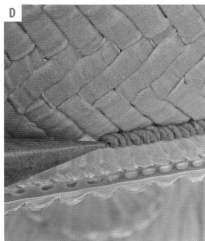

TRADITIONAL BASKETWEAVE

1 Mark a vertical line using a smooth edge cake scraper on the cake side to ensure your vertical basketweave lines are straight. You can judge the rest from this first line (A).

2 Using Wilton nozzle number 45, or 48, with the smooth side pointing upwards, pipe a vertical line. You can start at either the top or the bottom, whichever you find easier (B).

3 Pipe about 4–5cm (1½–2in) short horizontal lines across the vertical line starting from either the top or bottom of the cake. The spacing between the lines should be the same as the width of the nozzle's tip opening (C).

TIP

It can be tricky to pipe straight lines, especially on the side of a cake. We suggest you practise piping on a cake board held upright. Another effective tip is to drag the piping bag quickly – this makes the lines less wiggly.

TIP

To create a different effect while using the same basketweave technique, try using a simple medium round nozzle or just cut the tip off a piping bag to create a medium-size hole. Or use two or more different shades of the colour you have chosen.

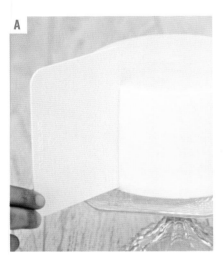

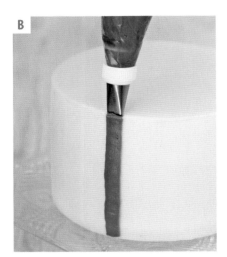

4 Pipe another vertical line that overlaps the horizontal lines. The spacing between the vertical lines should be less than 2.5cm (1in). Pipe another sets of horizontal lines and make sure each line is slightly buried under the first vertical line (D).

5 Repeat the process of piping vertical and horizontal lines until you cover the whole cake (E).

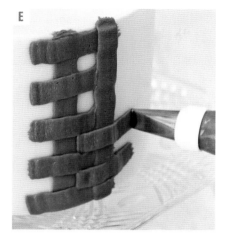

E

TIP
Make sure that you pipe the 'weaves' before the crumb coat has crusted and with a little pressure so they stick to your cake. The horizontal weaves should seem like they are coming from underneath the vertical weaves to make the basketweave look more realistic.

TO CREATE THIS CAKE...

- 15 x 15cm (6 x 6in) round cake
- 950g–1.25kg (2lb 2oz–2lb 12oz) buttercream
- Paste colours: turquoise (Sugarflair Turquoise), dark pink (Sugarflair Claret), light green (Sugarflair Bittermelon)
- Piping bags
- Basketweave nozzle (Wilton 48) or plain basketweave nozzle (Wilton 45) and small petal nozzle (Wilton 104)
- Side scraper or ruler
- Cake stand or covered cake board

Cover the cake (see Covering Cakes, Buttercream Basics), and place on a covered cake board or stand. Colour 400–500g (14oz–1lb 2oz) of buttercream turquoise, and 100–150g (3½–5½oz) a darker shade of turquoise. Pipe the basketweave pattern as described in the tutorial. Pipe a border using the crochet technique (see Crochet, Textile Effects) on the top edge of the cake with the darker shade of turquoise and a piping bag with the tip snipped off. Finish by piping camellias around the base using 400–500g (14oz–1lb 2oz) dark pink for the petals and 50–100g (1¾–3½oz) light green for the centres (see Camellia and Hydrangea, Piping Flowers).

E- AND C-SCROLLS

This is one of the easiest techniques to master, yet it can produce a really rather elegant design when nicely coordinated, the lavish swirls create a rich and elaborate texture. The two types are named after the letter of the alphabet that they resemble. We like to combine the e- and c-scrolls to achieve a Victorian look on a cake.

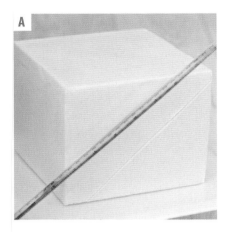

1 Using a ruler, mark 6.5–7.5cm (2½ –3in) wide diagonal bands on all sides of the cake (A).

2 Using a star nozzle (Wilton 16), pipe a reverse c-scroll by holding the piping bag straight on to the cake with the curve tip touching the surface (B). Squeeze with even pressure, and move a little to the left before circling up and around to the right, down and then and up, creating a backwards letter 'c'.

3 Pipe another c-scroll from the same starting point as the first, but this time do the opposite (C). The piping bag goes around to the left then up until it creates a 'c'.

4 Repeat the process until you finish piping inside all the diagonal bands (D).

5 Next, pipe continuous e-scrolls on top of the guide lines. Hold the piping bag straight on to the cake and with even pressure, squeeze the piping bag to the right and around creating a small 'e' shaped loop (E and F).

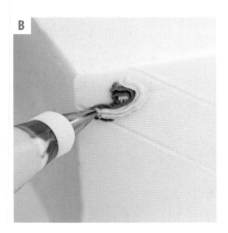

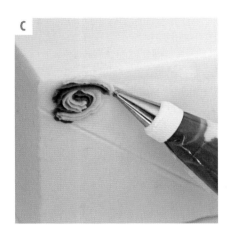

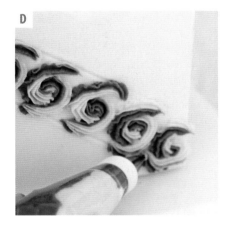

TO CREATE THIS CAKE...

- 20 x 15cm (8 x 6in) square cake (bottom tier), 15 x 10cm (6 x 4in) square cake (top tier)
- Dowel rods
- 1.4kg–1.8kg (3lb 1½oz–4lb) buttercream
- Paste colours: peach (Sugarflair Peach) and turquoise (Sugarflair Turquoise)
- Piping bags
- Star nozzle (Wilton 16)
- Palette knife
- Edible pearls (sugar balls)
- Tweezers
- Cake stand or covered cake board

Colour 600–800g (1lb 5oz–1lb 12oz) of buttercream peach, cover and smooth the cake (see Covering Cakes, Buttercream Basics) and place on a stand or covered board. Colour 400–500g (14oz–1lb 2oz) of buttercream turquoise, leave the rest uncoloured, and fill a piping bag to create a two-tone effect (see Up and Down Two-Tone Ruffles, Piping Textures and Patterns). Pipe the c- and e-scrolls as described in the tutorial. Pipe random scrolls in peach (see Scrolls, Lines and Zigzags, Piping Textures and Patterns) and stick on edible pearls using tweezers. Finally, pipe the bottom border using the crochet technique (see Crochet, Textile Effects).

STAR FILL

Forget about intricate patterns and complicated designs, for this star fill technique all you need to do is decide on a simple pattern, mark and pipe the outline, then fill it with stars. It couldn't be easier!

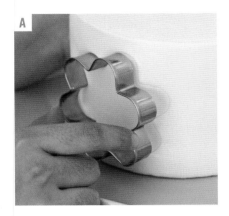

1 You can draw freehand or use cookie cutters to mark the outline of your patterns (A and B).

2 After doing so, pipe crochet effect (see Crochet, Textile Effects) to outline your designs. Make sure to use different colours from the ones you will use to make the star fill to do this.

3 Using a star nozzle (Wilton 16), position the nozzle straight on to cake and firmly squeeze the piping bag until the buttercream comes out and creates a star, then stop squeezing the bag and pull away abruptly (C).

4 Repeat the same process until the space inside the patterns are covered without any gaps (D).

TO CREATE THIS CAKE...

- 20 x 15cm (8 x 6in) round cake (bottom tier), 15 x 7.5cm (6 x 3in) round cake (top tier)
- Dowel rods
- 1.6–2.2kg (3lb 8oz–5lb) buttercream
- Paste colours: yellow-orange (Sugarflair Eyptian Orange), orange (Sugarflair Tangerine), light brown (Sugarflair Dark Brown), dark brown (Sugarflair Dark Brown)
- Star nozzle (Wilton 16)
- Piping bags
- Cocktail stick (tooth pick)
- Cake stand or covered board

Cover the top tier with 600–800g (1lb 5oz–1lb 12oz) yellow-orange buttercream and the bottom tier with 400–500g (14oz–1lb 2oz) orange, give them a smooth finish, then dowel and stack them (see Covering Cakes, Buttercream Basics). Place on a stand or covered board. Pipe the design following the tutorial, using 200–300g (7–10½oz) each of light brown, dark brown and plain buttercream, and the leftover orange and yellow-orange.

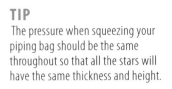

TIP
The pressure when squeezing your piping bag should be the same throughout so that all the stars will have the same thickness and height.

DOTS

Dots are similar to the star fill technique, but require less buttercream. With dots your design can be more precise because you have better control over the shape of your pattern since you will be outlining it with dots as well as filling it with dots. Yes, just dots.

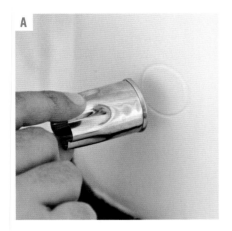

1 After smoothing the cake, use cookie cutters to mark patterns, or draw them with a cocktail stick (toothpick) (A and B).

2 Prepare all the colours you need in individual piping bags and use scissors to cut a tiny hole at the end of each bag. Outline your patterns with dots by holding the piping bag straight on to the cake, and gently squeezing the bag until a small dot appears (C). Make sure to stop squeezing the bag before you pull it away. It is best to outline patterns first before piping the inside of the patterns.

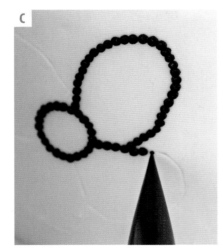

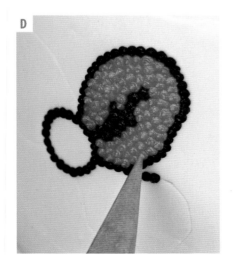

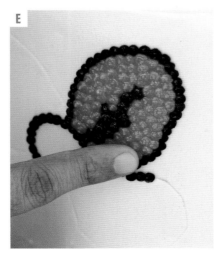

3 Repeat the same process and start filling the inside part of the patterns with your chosen colour, ensuring that you don't leave any gaps in between the dots (D).

4 Pipe a dotted line as a stem to connect flowers and leaves. Pipe some more dots as borders. If your dots have some 'spikes', wait until they have crusted then gently press the spiky points down (E).

TO CREATE THIS CAKE...

- 20 x 15cm (8 x 6in) round cake (bottom tier), 15 x 10cm (6 x 4in) round cake (top tier)
- Dowel rods
- 1.65–2.55kg (3lb 10oz–5lb 9oz) buttercream
- Paste colours: pink (Sugarflair Pink), yellow (Sugarflair Autumn Leaf), violet (Sugarflair Grape Violet), green (Sugarflair Spruce Green), light orange (Sugarflair Tangerine), dark orange (Sugarflair Tangerine), black (Sugarflair Liquorice)
- Cookie cutters (optional)
- Cocktail stick (toothpick)
- Piping bags
- Scissors
- Palette knife
- Cake stand or covered cake board

Crumb coat, dowel and stack the cakes (see Buttercream Basics) and place on a stand or covered board. Cover the cakes with 600–800g (1lb 5oz–1lb 12oz) of uncoloured buttercream and give them a smooth finish (see Covering Cakes, Buttercream Basics). Mark the surface with cookie cutters or draw your design freehand using a cocktail stick. Divide the remaining buttercream equally into seven parts and colour each one pink, yellow, violet, green, light orange, dark orange and black. Fill your piping bags and snip the ends off to make a small hole. Pipe your design following the tutorial.

LEAVES

If you think that piping leaves on a cake can only be used to accentuate the piped flowers or to cover imperfections, think again. By using a leaf nozzle, you can create a really striking texture on a cake. We've described two below, the first shows that simple plain lines become not so plain after all, and the second makes a fabulous spiked effect. You can use different colours to add visual interest.

1 For the first effect, using a small leaf nozzle (Wilton 352), hold the piping bag straight down with two points of the nozzle against the cake. Starting from the corner of the cake, gently squeeze the piping bag as you drag vertically upwards (A). When you reach the top edge of the cake, stop squeezing the bag and pull abruptly to leave a small peak.

2 Repeat process around the cake with 1–2cm (½–¾in) gaps between, using alternating colours of white and yellow (B).

3 For the second effect, mark a guide line to indicate a border 2.5cm (1in) wide at the top and bottom of your cake. Identify the middle of what will be the back of the cake by measuring the circumference and dividing in two. From this point, hold your piping bag at a 20–30 degree angle and squeeze the piping bag to create a row of five or six small leaves vertically. Repeat the process and pipe rows of leaves close to each until you get back to the middle part of the cake, making sure there are no gaps inbetween the leaves. Repeat the same process on to the other half of the cake (C).

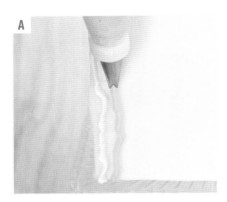

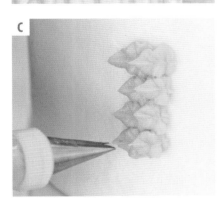

TIP
A small leaf nozzle (Wilton 352) is the only tool used to create these strikingly different textures. It all relies on how much pressure you put in squeezing your piping bag and the position of your nozzle. Do not forget to stop squeezing your piping bag before you pull it. Otherwise, you will have a long and funny-looking leaf.

4 To pipe a big sunflower-like flower, use a large leaf nozzle (Wilton 366) to pipe the petals (D), then cut the tip of a piping bag and pipe 'spikes' for the centre of the flower. This technique is described in more detail in the Piping Flowers chapter.

TO CREATE THIS CAKE...

- 15 x 13cm (6 x 5in) square cake (bottom tier), 15 x 10cm (6 x 4in) round cake (top tier)
- Dowel rods
- 1.15–1.55kg (2lb 9½–3lb 7oz) buttercream
- Paste colours: white (Sugarflair Super White), yellow (Sugarflair Melon and Autumn Leaf), teal (Sugarflair Eucalyptus)
- Piping bags
- Small leaf nozzle (Wilton 352)
- Large leaf nozzle (Wilton 366)
- Cocktail stick (toothpick)
- Ruler
- Scissors

Colour 400–500g (14oz–1lb 2oz) of buttercream yellow, 150–250g (5½–9oz) teal and the rest white. Cover both cakes in white buttercream and give them a smooth finish (see Covering Cakes, Buttercream Basics). Dowel and stack them (see Buttercream Basics) and place on a stand or covered board. For the bottom tier, pipe the first texture described in the tutorial in alternating yellow and white lines. For the top tier, pipe the second texture described above in yellow. Finish off the veritcal gap where you began your first row of leaves with a line of yellow dots (see Dots, Piping Textures and Patterns). Snip off the end off a piping bag to pipe dots in teal around the top and bottom edges. Using the large leaf nozzle (Wilton 366), pipe a large sunflower on the corner of the bottom tier in teal, adding dots in white buttercream for the centre (see Sunflower and Leaves, Piping Flowers).

SHELLS AND FLEUR-DE-LIS

The technique of piping shells and fleur-de-lis using a star tip has been done for many years, with shells commonly used as borders. But we will give it a twist. By using vibrant colours and combining the patterns in interesting ways, we will make this age-old technique into contemporary art.

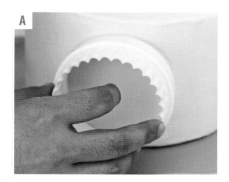

1 For our variation on basic shells, we have piped a stylized flower using the basic shell technique. To do this, use a round cookie cutter or a cup or glass that fits nicely on the side of your cake and mark a guide circle (A).

2 Pipe 'shells' using a star tip nozzle (Wilton 21) starting at the edge of the guide circle. Hold the piping bag straight onto the cake with tip of the nozzle touching the guide circle. Firmly squeeze the piping bag until the buttercream builds up and creates a fan shape, then slightly lift the piping bag and pull down towards the centre of the guide circle as you also gradually relax the pressure to create a pointed end (B). Pipe shells next to each other to finish one layer. Repeat the same process and pipe two more rows, each row getting shorter as it draws nearer to the centre of the circle (C).

3 For the fleur-de-lis, using small star nozzle (Wilton 16), pipe each one by starting with a reverse shell. Hold the piping bag straight on to the cake and pipe a short shell but pull your strokes *upwards,* not down (D). Then pipe another short shell that starts on the left side then curls slightly up then meets the central shell, do the same on the on the right. Both strokes join in the centre (E).

TIP
Use differently sized star nozzles to create various effects. To make your designs more interesting, use the two-tone technique as discussed earlier in the Piping Textures and Patterns chapter.

TO CREATE THIS CAKE...

- 15 x 15cm (6 x 6in) round cake
- 1.55–2.05kg (3lb 7oz–4lb 10oz) buttercream
- Paste colours: purple (Sugarflair Grape Violet), light orange (Sugarflair Tangerine), orange (Sugarflair Tangerine), dark orange (Sugarflair Tangerine)
- Piping bags
- Star nozzles (Wilton 16 and 21)
- Silver edible balls (sugar balls)
- Tweezers
- Cake stand or covered cake board

Colour 400–500g (14oz–1lb 2oz) of buttercream violet, and 250–350g (9–12oz) each in light orange, orange and dark orange and leave the rest plain. Cover the cake with plain buttercream (see Covering Cakes, Buttercream Basics) and place on a stand or covered board. Blend violet buttercream into the background coating at the top and bottom of the cake (see Blending, Palette Knife Techniques) and give the cake a smooth finish (see Covering Cakes, Buttercream Basics). Mark guide circles around your cake, spacing them evenly, then pipe the 'shell' flower following the tutorial using all the orange colours. Add silver edible balls in the centre using tweezers. Starting about 1.5cm (⅝in) from the bottom of the cake, pipe the fleur-de-lis in violet, following the tutorial, all around the base, and add one silver edible ball to the centre of each.

SCROLLS, LINES AND ZIGZAGS

In this technique you won't need any special tools, just a simple piping bag. We could call this technique 'line art' because just by piping curved and straight lines you will be able to create an illustration. This looks great on a nice, smooth and simple background that allows your design to really stand out.

1 Measure and cut greaseproof (wax) paper to create your pattern – here we've made equally spaced triangles – and mark them on your cake using a cocktail stick (toothpick) (A).

2 Put an ample amount of buttercream of different colours in separate piping bags and snip off the tip of each bag to create a small hole. Pipe on top of your guide all around the cake in one colour, then use the rest of the colours alternately until you cover the whole surface of the cake with zigzag lines (B).

3 To make floral patterns, use flower or petal cookie cutters, positioning them on to the cake and mark your guide lines (C). Pipe around the guide then pipe some repetitive lines in different directions to fill the spaces of your pattern. It is nice to mix some straight and curve lines (D). After filling the main pattern, pipe some freehand repetitive bigger scrolls to complement the structured patterns of the main flower.

TO CREATE THIS CAKE...

- 15 x 15cm (6 x 6in) round cake (top tier), 20 x 7.5cm (8 x 3in) round cake (bottom tier)
- Dowel rods
- 1.45–1.85kg (3lb 3½oz–4lb 2oz) buttercream
- Paste colours: green (Sugarflair Gooseberry), grey (Sugarflair Liquorice), black (Sugarflair Liquorice)
- Piping bags
- Cookie cutters
- Ruler
- Greaseproof (wax) paper
- Cocktail stick (toothpick)
- Scissors
- Cake stand or covered board

Colour 600–700g (1lb 5oz–1lb 9oz) of buttercream green, 400–500g (14oz–1lb 2oz) grey, 250–350g (9–12oz) black and leave the rest uncoloured. Cover the top tier with green buttercream and the bottom with grey, reserving some of the green and grey to pipe the lines on the lower tier, then give both cakes a smooth finish (see Covering Cakes, Buttercream Basics). Dowel and stack them (see Buttercream Basics) and place on a stand or covered cake board. Measure the circumference of the bottom tier cake and calculate the size you need for equal triangles. Mark them on the cake and pipe lines following the tutorial, starting with black and using the other colours alternately until the cake is covered. On the top tier, pipe the floral designs in the same way, adding repetitive lines to fill. Pipe some freehand scrolls between the shapes. Finish by piping dots (see Dots, Piping Textures and Patterns) around the upper and lower border of the top tier.

A

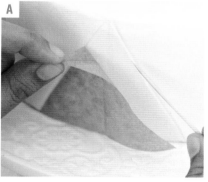

B

C

D

TIP
To practise squeezing your piping bag with constant pressure, we suggest that you pipe scribbles on a plate, glass or any board. Fantastic sources of inspirations for piped patterns include tribal art, 'Zentangle', and Aztec patterns to name a few.

PIPING FLOWERS

There is almost nothing more popular than a floral theme
on a cake. Despite their apparent intricacy, flowers
of all sorts can be piped in buttercream, which lends
itself very well to creating delicate petals and foliage.
In this chapter we will show you how to pipe a rich
variety of flowers, from the essential rose, to flamboyant
chrysanthemums and a posy of cottage garden favourites.

SUNFLOWER AND LEAVES

With their vibrant and cheery yellow petals, sunflowers can brighten your day, whether they are planted in your garden or piped on a cake. This is a very easy flower to create and works equally well as a decoration for the top of a cupcake or as a feature on a larger cake. A few green leaves will really set off the bright petals, and the following Leaves tutorial can be used to add foliage to any floral design.

SUNFLOWER

1 Using a piping bag with a writing nozzle, pipe a circle as a guide to the size of your flower (A).

2 Using a small leaf nozzle (Wilton 352), position the nozzle at a 20 to 30 degree angle and have one of the points touching your guide circle. Squeeze your piping bag until it creates a wide base then gently pull away, slowly decreasing the pressure on the bag as you do so (B).

3 When you reach the desired length of the petal, stop squeezing your bag then pull abruptly. Repeat this process to pipe petals all the way around the circle (C).

4 Pipe another layer of petals at a slightly steeper angle than the first (30 to 40 degrees), making sure that they are close to the first layer of petals to avoid gaps. Ideally, you should pipe these petals between those of the first layer (D). Finally, using brown tinted buttercream, pipe little dots in the centre of the flower (E).

TIP
You can also use Oreo cookies, chocolate sprinkles or any similar edible goodies, to fill the middle of the sunflower.

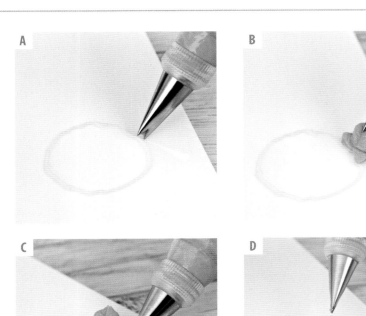

Sunflowers are the first flowers that we ever learned to pipe in buttercream and remain one of our favourites for their simplicity and striking style. They look so effective when piped singly or in pairs on cupcakes. To achieve the raised effect in the centre of the double-bloom cupcakes, pipe a blob of uncoloured buttercream in the centre of the cupcake first, then pipe two sunflowers on opposite sides. Sunflowers can also be combined on a cake to create a masterpiece worthy of Van Gogh himself! See the Cupcake Bouquet tutorial later in this chapter to see just how effective these flowers can look *en masse*.

LEAVES

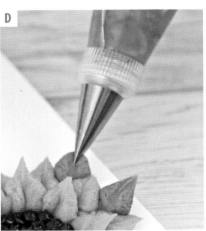

1 Using the same method as for the petals of the sunflower, use a small leaf nozzle (Wilton 352). Choose a point below the outer layer of petals and position your nozzle so it is at a 20 to 30 degree angle with one point touching the cake (A).

2 Squeeze your piping bag until it creates a wide base then gently pull away to create the leaf (B).

3 When you reach the desired length of the leaf, which for a sunflower will be about the same length as the petals, stop squeezing your bag then pull abruptly (C).

4 Repeat this process to pipe leaves at intervals around the flower (D).

TO CREATE THIS CAKE...

- 20 x 10cm (8 x 4in) round cake, or a dozen cupcakes
- 500–750g (1lb 2oz–1lb 10oz) buttercream
- Paste colours: yellow (Sugarflair Melon and Autumn Leaf) brown (Sugarflair Chestnut), mocha (Sugarflair Dark Brown) and green (Spruce Green)
- Piping bags
- Cake stand or covered cake board
- Small leaf nozzle (Wilton 352)
- Writing nozzle 1 or 2 (optional)

Plan the layout of your flowers, using paintings and photographs as inspiration, to achieve a balanced look. Cover the cake with plain buttercream and a smooth finish (see Covering Cakes, Buttercream Basics) and place on a stand or covered board. Colour 200–300g (7–10½oz) of buttercream yellow, and 100–150g (3½–5½oz) each of brown, mocha and green. Pipe the sunflowers and leaves as described in the tutorials then pipe some trailing stems in green with a writing nozzle.

CAMELLIA AND HYDRANGEA

Camellias and hydrangeas can both be piped straight on to a cake or a cupcake, and use the same piping principle. Camellia is a flower that you can pipe using a minimal amount of buttercream but gives an extraordinary look. The individual elements of a hydrangea bloom form a flowerhead which resembles a large pompom, and is an absolute eye catcher.

CAMELLIA

1 Pipe a guide circle the same size as you want your flower to be. Using a small petal nozzle (Wilton 104), position your nozzle with the wide end touching the guide circle. Hold the bag at a 20 to 30 degree angle and, without moving your piping bag, give it a good squeeze until the buttercream creates a fan shape. Stop squeezing then gently pull towards you. This will be the first in your outer row of petals (A).

2 Repeat the same process to pipe another layer of petals (B). Make sure that the piping bag is really close to your first layer so there are no gaps. Depending on how big your flower is, you might need to pipe few more layers of petals.

3 Use green tinted buttercream to pipe some spikes in the middle then yellow tinted buttercream to pipe dots to give a create a realistic flower centre (C).

4 Pipe some leaves using a leaf nozzle (see Sunflower and Leaves, Piping Flowers) (D).

TIP
When piping petals, all you have to do is position your nozzle at the right angle and remember these three words: squeeze...stop...pull.

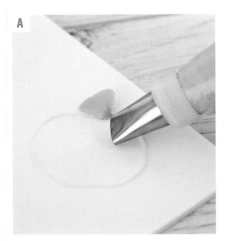

A

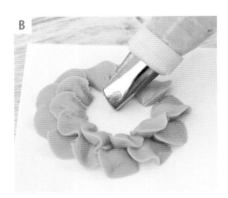

B

C

D

Aside from using fancy cupcake cases (liners), a clever alternative for a floral theme are these silicone plant pots, which you can buy from many cake supply shops, especially the larger online retailers. This will give a real 'garden' look to your cupcakes. Rather than giving your cupcakes a plain smooth covering, you can add more interest by piping ruffles (see Piping Textures and Patterns) around the edge before you add your flowers on top. Choose a colour that will compliment your flowers. We have found that this light green usually works well.

HYDRANGEA

1 Fill your piping bag with two colours of buttercream (see the two-tone effect in Up and Down Two-Tone Ruffles, Piping Textures and Patterns). Using a small petal nozzle (Wilton 103), hold the bag at a 20 to 30 degree angle with the wide end of the nozzle touching the surface, then give it a good squeeze until you create a fan shape. Stop squeezing the bag and then gently pull it towards you (A).

2 Repeat the same process and pipe three more petals making sure that all petals will start at one common point (B).

3 Pipe clusters of flowers to create the flowerhead of a hydrangea. Use green tinted buttercream to pipe dots in the centre of each of the flowers (C).

4 Pipe some leaves using a leaf nozzle (see Sunflower and Leaves) (D).

TO CREATE THIS CAKE...

- 15 x 13cm (6 x 5in) square cake
- 1.45–2.05kg (3lb 3½oz–4lb 10oz) buttercream
- Paste colours: light yellow-green, (Sugarflair Melon and Gooseberry), light blue (Sugarflair Baby Blue), light green (Sugarflair Gooseberry), orange (Sugarflair Egyptian Orange), yellow (Sugarflair Autumn Leaf)
- Piping bags
- Petal nozzles (Wilton 103 and 104)
- Side scraper or ruler
- Scissors
- Cake stand or covered cake board

Crumb coat the cake (see Buttercream Basics) and place on a stand or covered cake board. Cover the cake with 500–600g (1lb 2oz–1lb 5oz) of light yellow-green tinted buttercream and smooth the surface (see Covering Cakes, Buttercream Basics). Colour the rest of the buttercream in the following quantities: 150–250g (5½–9oz) each of light blue, light green and yellow, and 250–350g (9–12oz) orange. Leave 250–350g (9–12oz) of buttercream uncoloured. Pipe the camellias on the corners in orange with yellow centres, following the camellia tutorial. Pipe hydrangeas on the top edges and corners using light blue and plain for the petals and green for the flower centres, following the tutorial. Finish by piping shells along the base of the cake in light yellow-green (see Shells and Fleur-de-lis, Piping Patterns and Textures).

A

B

C

D

TIP
Piping hydrangeas is easy, you just need to connect all four petals at one central point. To make them more realistic, use the two-tone effect (see Up and Down Two-Tone Ruffles, Piping Textures and Patterns). And don't forget the magic words: squeeze... stop... pull!

CARNATION AND SWEET PEA

These two garden favourites are further examples of easy-to-pipe flowers. Both are always in season when it comes to cake decoration, and are the perfect choice for both full-size cakes and cupcakes. Sweet peas make a good alternative if you want something different from swirls, and they are also good 'filler flowers' for a more elaborate floral arrangement.

CARNATION

1 Create a two-tone effect by filling a piping bag (with attached small petal nozzle, Wilton 104) with two desired colours of buttercream in separate bags (see Up and Down Two-Tone Ruffles, Piping Textures and Patterns). The 'stripe' colour will be the one in the narrow end of the nozzle.

2 Using a piping bag with a writing nozzle, pipe a circle as a guide to the size of your flower. With the nozzle at a 20 to 30 degree angle and the wider end touching the surface (A), continuously squeeze the piping bag as you move it slightly up and down to create wavy petals. Pipe a circular row of petals following the guide circle (B).

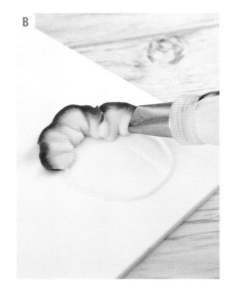

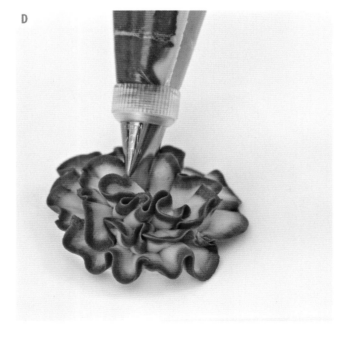

3 Pipe another row of petals, starting slightly inside the first circle, with the wide end of the nozzle held at a 30 to 40 degree angle and touching the first row of petals (C).

4 Repeat the same process to create several layers of petals until you fill the middle of the flower and create a domed shape (D).

TIP
A carnation uses a lot of buttercream and is quite heavy, therefore it is not advisable to pipe one on the side of a cake where there is no support. It is best to pipe it on a corner, bottom or on a flat surface.

The frilly two-tone petals of a carnation make the perfect decoration for a cupcake and are much more exciting and original than your average swirl. When paired with cupcakes in pink paper cases and pretty vintage china they make a real statement – experiment with colours that go well with your own vintage crockery. A simple ruffle effect was piped round the edge of this cupcake in pink buttercream first (see Piping Textures and Patterns) before piping the carnation in the centre and then the leaves (see Sunflower and Leaves earlier in this chapter).

SWEET PEA

1 Using a small petal nozzle (Wilton 104), position it at a 20 to 30 degree angle with the wide end of the nozzle touching the surface of the cake or cupcake and narrow end pointing out. Keep the nozzle steady and moderately squeeze the piping bag until it creates a fan shape petal (A).

2 Repeat the same process to pipe another petal next to the first, but make sure you allow sufficient space so that when you pipe the second petal it does not overlap the first (B).

3 Pipe two smaller petals starting at the base of the bigger petals (C).

4 Pipe the stem and calyx with green tinted buttercream using a writing nozzle 1 or 2, or a piping bag with the tip snipped off (D).

TIP

If you do not have a writing nozzle, you can just snip the very top off the piping bag with a pair of scissors to leave a very small hole.

TO CREATE THIS CAKE...

- 15 x 10cm (6 x 4in) round cake (bottom tier), 10 x 7.5cm (4 x 3in) round cake (top tier), or a dozen cupcakes
- 1.1–1.7kg (2lb 7½oz–3lb 12oz) buttercream
- Paste colours: dark pink (Sugarflair Claret), pale green (Sugarflair Gooseberry) and dark green (Sugarflair Spruce Green)
- Piping bags
- Cake stand or covered cake board
- Small petal nozzle (Wilton 104)
- Small leaf nozzle (Wilton 352)
- Writing nozzle, l or 2
- Scissors

Crumb coat, dowel and stack the cakes (see Buttercream Basics) and place on a stand or covered board. Cover the top tier with 200–300g (7–10½oz) of plain buttercream and the bottom tier with 300–400g (10½–14½oz) of pale green buttercream, and give them a smooth finish (see Covering Cakes, Buttercream Basics). Pipe vertical lines of dots in pale green on the bottom tier (see Dots, Piping Textures and Patterns). Colour 100–200g (3½–7oz) of buttercream dark pink and 200–300g (7–10½oz) dark green. Pipe sweet peas round the top tier following the tutorial. Next colour 100–200g (3½–7oz) of buttercream dark pink and fill a piping bag with this and 200–300g (7–10½oz) of uncoloured buttercream to create a two-tone effect. Pipe a large carnation on the top of the cake following the tutorial. Use the remaining dark green buttercream to add the leaves (see Sunflower and Leaves, Piping Flowers) around the carnation.

LILAC AND DAISY

Lilacs are popular flowers that make an excellent choice for borders, with the added advantage that they do a great job of hiding cake imperfections. Daisies define simplicity at its best. We think that it is the easiest flower to pipe and is an excellent alternative to massive swirls and peaks.

LILAC

1 Using a small petal nozzle (Wilton 104), position the nozzle at a 20 to 30 degree angle with the wide end of the nozzle pointing downwards (A). Squeeze the piping bag with even pressure and follow a tight U-shape, without the space in the middle, until you create a small petal (B).

2 Repeat the same process and pipe three more petals making sure that they all start at one common point and that there isn't a big gap in the centre (C).

3 Cut the tip off a piping bag and use yellow-tinted buttercream to pipe dots in the centre of each of the flowers (D).

4 Pipe some leaves using a leaf nozzle (see Sunflower and Leaves) (E).

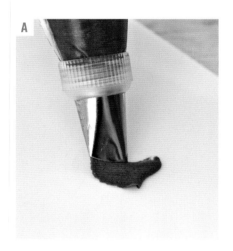

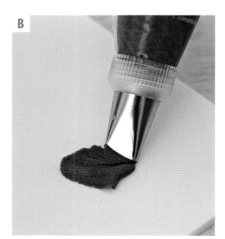

TIP
Try using the two-tone effect described in the Ruffles section of Piping Textures and Patterns. Since these flowers use a small amount of buttercream, they are not heavy so you can pipe them on the sides of the cake. Just make sure you use a bit of pressure as you pipe so that they stick to the cake.

Sweetly pretty, lilac and daisies make a lovely combination resulting in a vintage mini bouquet. For variety, decorate some cupcakes with just a single daisy and others with both flowers. By keeping it simple with these two blooms you can pipe lots of cupcakes, perhaps together with a main cake to complement them, in a relatively short time — ideal if you are preparing for a celebration party with a big guest list. Why not dress the party table with fresh flowers, including lilac and daisies to match your cakes? The effect would be stunning!

DAISY

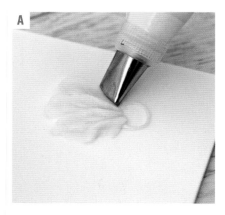

1 Pipe a small guide circle, then using a small petal nozzle (Wilton 104), position the nozzle flat to the surface of the cake with the wide end facing towards you. Continuously squeeze the piping bag with even pressure and follow a long U-shape, but without the space in the middle of the 'U', until you create a small petal.

2 Repeat the same process and pipe more petals (A), allowing them to overlap a little, and making sure that they all meet at one common point and don't leave a big gap in the centre. Continue until you have completed the circle of petals (B).

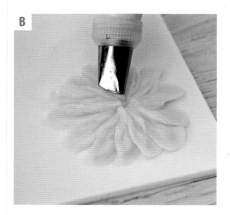

3 To pipe the centre of the flower, cut the tip off the piping bag and, using yellow-tinted buttercream, pipe in a continuous circular motion with even pressure, until the spiral creates a dome (C).

4 Pipe some leaves using a leaf nozzle (see Sunflower and Leaves, Piping Flowers) (D).

TO CREATE THIS CAKE...

- 15 x 10cm (6 x 4in) round cake
- 1.3–2kg (3lb–4lb 8oz) buttercream
- Paste colours: light chestnut (Sugarflair Chestnut), dark chestnut (Sugarflair Chestnut), violet, (Sugarflair Grape Violet), light green (Sugarflair Gooseberry), orange (Sugarflair Egyptian Orange), yellow (Sugarflair Autumn Leaf)
- Piping bags
- Small petal nozzle (Wilton 104)
- Leaf nozzle (Wilton 352)
- Palette knife
- Scissors
- Cake stand or covered cake board

Crumb coat the cake (see Buttercream Basics) and place on a stand or covered cake board. Cover the cake with 300–400g (10½–14oz) of light chestnut buttercream and use a palette knife and 100–200g (3½–7oz) of dark chestnut buttercream to create a streaked effect (see Blending, Palette Knife Techniques). Colour the remaining buttercream in the following quantities: 150–250g (5½–9oz) each of violet, light green and yellow, 250–350g (9–12oz) orange and leave 200–300g (7–10½oz) uncoloured. Pipe the daisies first with plain petals and yellow centres, then the violets with violet petals and orange centres, following the relevant tutorials above. Pipe some leaves between the flowers in light green (see Sunflower and Leaves, Piping Flowers).

TIP

For the daisy, your nozzle needs to be completely flat on the surface and you must start from the centre of the flower. Just remember these three words: squeeze, up and down! For the flower centre, you can either pipe a dome or use chocolates or candies for an interesting touch.

CHRYSANTHEMUM AND DAFFODIL

Chrysanthemums are mostly known for their vibrant colours and shape. Adding them gives a much bolder and more daring look to a cake than some of the more conservative flowers. Creating chrysanthemums involves a repeated piping action which delivers excellent results. Daffodils too are very popular flowers, ideal for a spring time cake, and despite the 'trumpet' at their centre they actually involve a very easy piping technique.

CHRYSANTHEMUM

1 Start by piping a guide circle. Using a chrysanthemum nozzle (Wilton 81), position the nozzle at a 20 to 30 degree angle with the curved end down and against the guide circle. Gently squeeze the piping bag with even pressure while pulling out with a quick stroke until you reach the desired length of petal – about 5mm (¼in). Repeat the process to create one layer of petals (A).

2 Repeat the same process and pipe two or more layers of petals. Make sure you pipe the succeeding petals in between the first row (B).

3 Cut the tip of the piping bag and use plain buttercream to pipe spikes in the centre of each of the flowers by holding the piping bag at a 90 degree angle and squeezing it until the buttercream creates a vertical line, then release the squeeze before pulling the bag away abruptly (C).

4 Pipe some leaves using a leaf nozzle (see Sunflower and Leaves, Piping Flowers) (D).

TIP
Make sure that you pipe the petals really close to each other so that you cannot see any gaps in between. This flower can be piped on the side of the cake but be careful not to make it too big because this will make it heavy and it could potentially fall off.

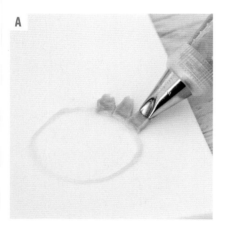

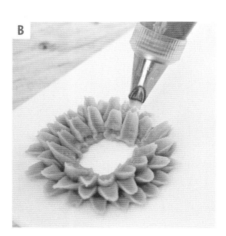

Daffodils are one of the first signs that spring has arrived, while chrysanthemums bloom at the end of summer, so these flowers are plucked from different seasons — but in cake decorating you're the boss and you can do what you like! No one could argue that the sunny daffodil and the rich and exciting colours of the chrysanthemum don't belong together on a pretty cake stand, especially when they are presented in these cute spotted cups. For these two flowers, the bigger they are the better because the form is more obvious when the petals are larger. Chrysanthemum nozzles come in different sizes, so go ahead and experiment with them.

DAFFODIL

1 Pipe a guide circle and 'points' to help you position the petals evenly (A).

2 Using a small petal nozzle (Wilton 104), position the nozzle at a 20 to 30 degree angle with wide end pointing down. While continuously squeezing the piping bag, move the nozzle up (B) then turn it to the right and back down until you create a long petal (C). Make sure there is no gap in the middle. Repeat the same process and pipe a total of five or six petals.

3 Cut the tip off a piping bag and use slightly darker yellow-tinted buttercream to pipe an overlapping spiral as the centre of the flower, about 1–1.5cm (½– ⅝in) tall (D).

4 Pipe some leaves using a leaf nozzle (see Sunflower and Leaves) (E).

TO CREATE THIS CAKE...

- 20 x 10cm (8 x 4in) round cake (bottom tier), 15 x 10cm (6 x 4in) round cake (top tier)
- Dowel rods
- 1.8–2.5kg (4lb–5lb 8oz) buttercream
- Paste colours: light yellow, (Sugarflair Melon and Autumn Leaf), mid yellow (Sugarflair Melon and Autumn Leaf), pink (Sugarflair Pink), orange (Sugarflair Egyptian Orange), light green (Sugarflair Gooseberry), dark yellow (Sugarflair Autumn Leaf), dark green (Sugarflair Spruce Green)
- Piping bags
- Petal nozzle (Wilton 104)
- Leaf nozzle (Wilton 352)
- Chrysanthemum nozzle (Wilton 81)
- Scalloped cake comb
- Scissors
- Cake stand or covered cake board

Crumb coat, dowel and stack the cakes (see Buttercream Basics) and place on a stand or covered cake board. Cover the cakes with 600–700g (1lb 5oz–1lb 9oz) of light yellow tinted buttercream, giving the top tier a smooth finish and the bottom one a ridged finish with the cake comb (see Buttercream Basics, Covering Cake). Colour the remaining buttercream in the following quantities 250–350g (9–12oz) each of mid yellow, pink and orange, and 150–250g (5½–9oz) each of light green, dark green and dark yellow. Pipe the flowers according to the tutorials, using mid yellow and dark yellow for the daffodils and orange and pink for the chrysanthemums. Add some stems in light green and leaves in dark green (see Sunflower and Leaves, Piping Flowers).

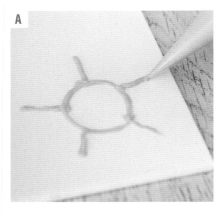

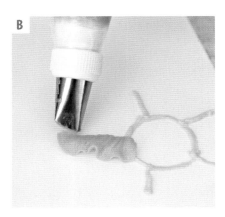

TIP
With daffodil petals, you just have to follow a long 'U' shape without a gap in the middle. Make sure you pipe five petals or your flower won't look right.

ROSE AND ROSE BUD

Roses are undeniably the most popular flower of all. Often described as the symbol of love, a rose never fails to touch someone's heart. A single rose on a cupcake or a cake says it all. How much more will a bouquet of roses express? With sufficient practice, you can master how to pipe truly realistic buttercream roses that will create a stunning effect.

ROSE

1 If you are piping the rose directly on a cupcake, you can pipe the bud straight on without piping a base. Use a petal nozzle (Wilton 104), which should be positioned vertically with the wide end touching the surface and slightly tilted inward. As you squeeze the piping bag with continuous, even pressure, turn the cupcake clockwise and make both ends of your buttercream bud meet (A). Make sure that the bud will only have a small opening.

2 While the nozzle is still slightly tilted inwards, pipe an arch shaped petal (as you also turn your cupcake) that goes around the bud, making sure that as you pipe you are also slightly pushing the petal against the bud so there are no gaps and it will not collapse. Each petal should start slightly past the middle of one petal and overlap the previous one. Pipe about two to four short petals (B).

3 After creating a bud with few petals around it, turn the nozzle straight then pipe a couple of slightly longer and higher 'arches' (C and D). Pipe about two to four petals. When piping last few petals, tilt the nozzle slightly outwards and make the arches longer instead of higher. Pipe about four to five petals (E).

4 Pipe leaves using a leaf nozzle (see Sunflower and Leaves, Piping Flowers) (F).

> **TIP**
> The secret for piping realistic roses is in the angle of your nozzle and the height of the 'arches'. Make sure also that you pipe the petals close to each other so they do not have any gaps and they will not easily break when you position them on your cake.

> **TIP**
> We do not advise you to try to put roses on the side of a cake where there is no support because they are heavy and will eventually fall off.

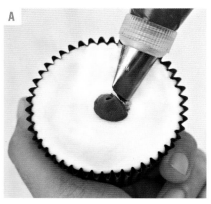
A

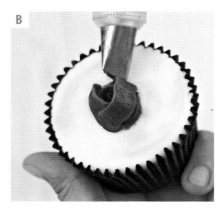
B

C

D

E

F

The trick with piping roses is to know when to stop piping the 'arches' and start piping the outer petals. Don't make the mistake of making your roses too huge – try to have them just the right size so that they provide just the right amount of buttercream in each mouthful. If the edges of your petals are breaking, chill the piping bag full of buttercream in the fridge for a few minutes and then massage the bag as if you were mixing the frosting. A two-tone effect will make your rose petals more realistic. For instructions on how to fill a piping bag with two colours see Up and Down Two-Tone Ruffles, Piping Textures and Patterns.

MAKING ROSES IN ADVANCE

If you want several roses on your cake, you will need either to make them in advance and freeze them, or pipe them on a flat surface or a flower nail (A), then 'lift' them with scissors in order to position them on your cake (B). For the freezing method, pipe a blob of buttercream on a flower nail, put a small piece of greaseproof (wax) paper on top then pipe the rose. Transfer to a tray and freeze.

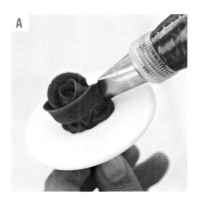

A

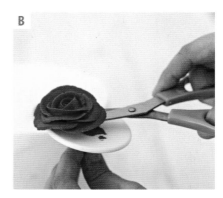

B

ROSE BUD

1 Using a small petal nozzle (Wilton 104), position the nozzle flat on the surface with the opening facing to the left. Gently squeeze the piping bag until it creates half a petal then pull the nozzle slightly out (to the right) and up then fold towards the centre.

2 Pipe an overlapping petal by holding the bag with the nozzle touching the upper edge of the first petal. Gently squeeze the piping bag and pull the nozzle slightly out (to the left) and up, then fold until it overlaps the first petal.

3 Depending on how big you want your bud to be, you can repeat steps 1 and 2 to add few more petals. When done, use scissors to cut the tip off a piping bag filled with green-tinted buttercream to pipe the calyx.

4 Pipe some leaves using a leaf nozzle (see Sunflower and Leaves, Piping Flowers).

TIP

Unlike roses, rose buds are always piped directly on the cake, and look particularly beautiful cascading down or growing up the sides of a cake. You can also use the two-tone effect described in the Up and Down Two-Tone Ruffles section of Piping Textures and Patterns.

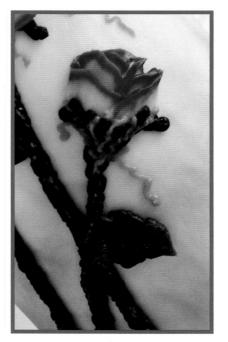

TO CREATE THIS CAKE...

- 10 x 20cm (4 x 8in) round cake
- 950g–1.45kg (2lb 2oz–3lb 3¼oz) buttercream
- Paste colours: light blue green, (Sugarflair Eucalyptus), dark pink (Sugarflair Dusky Pink), dark green (Sugarflair Spruce Green), light green (Sugarflair Gooseberry)
- Piping bags
- Small petal nozzle (Wilton 104)
- Leaf nozzle (Wilton 352)
- Cake scraper or ruler
- Palette knife
- Scissors
- Cake stand or covered cake board

Crumb coat then cover the cake with 200–300g (7–10½oz) of plain buttercream and blend using 100–200g (3½–7oz) light blue green from the base up (see Blending, Palette Knife Techniques). Smooth the cake (see Smoothing, Buttercream Basics). Colour 100–200g (3½–7oz) buttercream dark pink, 200–300g (7–10½oz) dark green and 100–150g (3½–5½oz) light green. Pipe the roses, following the tutorial, using dark pink and 250–300g (9–10½oz) plain buttercream for a two-tone effect (see Up and Down Two-Tone Ruffles, Piping Textures and Patterns). Pipe a rose bud in the same colours following the tutorial. Pipe stems in dark green using the crochet technique (see Crochet, Textile Effects). Add leaves in dark green (see Sunflower and Leaves, Piping Flowers) and tendrils in light green.

PIPING AND ARRANGING FLOWERS ON A CAKE

Now that you have learned how to pipe a whole garden-full of buttercream flowers, you can become a florist and arrange them on a cake. Here are four techniques you can use in order to position them securely and at the desired angle, to create just the look that you want. Anyone would be delighted to receive a beautiful bouquet of flowers – even more so if they are edible!

1 To securely attach a flower: Pipe some roses in advance and use the freezing method described in the Roses tutorial. Ideally, roses should be the first flowers to be positioned on a cake. Decide where you want them and using a piping bag with a simple round nozzle (or just snip off the end of the piping bag), continuously squeeze the bag to create a blob. Peel off a rose from the greaseproof (wax) paper and quickly rest it on the blob (A). A palette knife and scissors can help you to tweak the position. Hold the sides of the rose and slightly twist as you press down to make sure that it sticks to the blob securely so it won't fall off.

2 To position a flower at a desired angle: Using a piping bag with a simple round nozzle (or just snip off the end of the piping bag), pipe a blob big and wide enough to create a flat surface for the flower to sit on. Make the blob high enough to raise the flower up to the right height (B), and pipe your flowers onto the raised blobs (C, D, E).

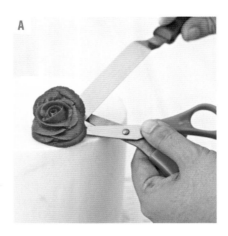

A

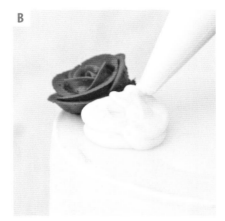

B

C

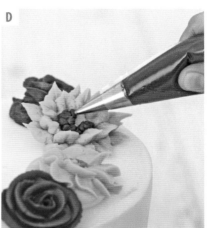

D

TIP

If positioning several flowers, pipe a guide circle on the surface of the cake to ensure your blobs, and therefore your flowers, are evenly spaced. When decorating a cake with a number of flowers on top you can simply crumb coat the top of the cake and add the flowers straight on top of that. There is no need to give the top a second layer of smooth buttercream as there is a tendency to use a lot of buttercream in the piping of the flowers and it can all become a bit too much!

E

3 To pipe flowers on the side of the cake: Make sure that you apply a little more pressure when you are piping, so that you are sure that the flowers stick to the cake. Avoid piping heavy flowers that use a lot of buttercream, such as carnations, on the side of a cake as they will sag or simply fall off.

4 To use flowers as fillers: You can pipe small flowers like hydrangeas, sweet peas and violets as well as leaves to cover up the blobs and to fill the gaps between flowers (F). Don't pipe all the leaves in the same shade of green, but prepare several different shades to make the results more realistic.

TO CREATE THIS CAKE...

- 15 x 10cm (6 x 4in) round cake
- 1.05–1.75kg (1lb 4oz–3lb 12oz) buttercream
- Paste colours: dark pink (Sugarflair Claret), light pink (Sugarflair Pink), red (Sugarflair Ruby Red), orange (Sugarflair Tangerine), purple (Sugarflair Grape Violet), green (Sugarflair Spruce Green or Gooseberry) and brown (Sugarflair Dark Brown)
- Piping bags
- Cake stand or covered cake board
- Small petal nozzles (Wilton 104)
- Small leaf nozzles (Wilton 352)
- Scissors

Cover the cake using plain buttercream and giving it a smooth finish (see Covering Cakes, Buttercream Basics) and place on a stand or covered board. Colour 150–250g (5½–9oz) of buttercream in each of the following colours: dark pink, light pink, red, orange, purple, green and brown. First pipe the roses, then the sunflower, chrysanthemum, carnation, sweet pea and finally the hydrangea and leaves according to the tutorials in this chapter, and bearing in mind the advice on arranging buttercream flowers on a cake. Complete the cake by piping a border around the base (see Shells and Fleur-de-lis, Piping Textures and Patterns).

CUPCAKE BOUQUET

A 'cupcake bouquet' is the way we describe a flower arrangement made of colour-coordinated, divine-tasting cupcakes. It is the perfect picture of an edible work of art and makes a stunning centrepiece or a lovely gift for any occasion. The key element used here is either a polystyrene (Styrofoam) ball, or several plastic cups. The cup method benefits from very easy to source materials, but both yield lovely results. Be a little playful when choosing your decoration and use different coloured papers and various accents.

STYROFOAM BALL METHOD

1 Place the Styrofoam ball into a flower pot and secure it with a glue or sticky tape. You may cover your pot with pretty fabric or leave it plain. Tie around some matching ribbons (A).

2 Place two cocktail sticks (toothpicks) in each position where you want a cupcake. The angle of the toothpicks should be about 30 to 45 degrees to support the cupcakes (B).

3 Arrange and stick your cupcake onto each pair of cocktail sticks. You may adjust the cocktail sticks as necessary to position the cupcakes close together and make sure as much of the Styrofoam ball is covered as possible (C). Your cupcakes can be ready decorated before you arrange them, however, to avoid damaging your piped buttercream flowers, it's best to pipe them after the cupcakes are arranged (D).

4 Fill any gaps with ruffled paper, fabrics, ribbons or pipe something into the gaps. You can also insert a florist's card holder for your message.

TO CREATE THIS BOUQUET...

- 12–15 cupcakes, standard size
- 430–570g (15¼oz–1lb 4¾oz) buttercream
- Paste colours: yellow (Sugarflair Melon and Autumn Leaf), brown (Sugarflair Dark Brown), green (Sugarflair Spruce Green)
- Styrofoam ball (whole or hemisphere)
- Flowerpot
- Fabric to cover pot
- Tissue paper
- Cocktail stick (toothpick)
- Ribbon
- Glue/sticky tape
- Scissors
- Florist's card holder (optional)

Choose a monochrome fabric to cover your flowerpot and black tissue for the styrofoam ball. Cover the cupcakes with 150–200g (5½–7oz) of plain buttercream. Colour the remaining buttercream in the following quantities: 130–150g (4½–5½oz) yellow, 100–150g (3½–5½oz) brown and 50–70g (1¾–2½oz) green. Follow the tutorial to assemble the bouquet. Pipe the sunflowers and leaves following the tutorial in the Piping Flowers chapter, adding the leaves at the end to fill in any spaces between the cupcakes.

TIP

The decorated cupcakes can make your bouquet top-heavy and therefore unstable. Unless you are using a heavy clay flowerpot, we suggest you add weight to the base by including a bag of pebbles or something similar.

CUP METHOD

1 Join seven plastic cups together with clear sticky tape to form the base for the bouquet (A). You can use more than seven cups, depending on how big you want your bouquet to be. Put some rolled sticky tape under the cups and stick them to a paper plate (B).

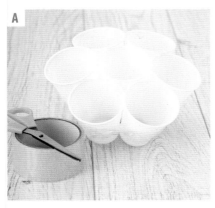

2 Put some rolled sticky tape around your cups so it is easier to stick the tissue paper around (C). You can use any material you can think of – coloured cellophane is also a nice option. When you have covered your base, tie a ribbon of your choice around it.

3 Cut the tissue paper into big squares, we used 20 x 20cm (8 x 8in) for a bouquet of seven cupcake. Put the squares inside each cup (D). The tissue paper will prevent your cupcakes from disappearing down inside if they are a little too small for the cups.

4 Lastly, arrange your floral cupcakes on your base and accentuate with artificial, sugar or large piped buttercream leaves (E).

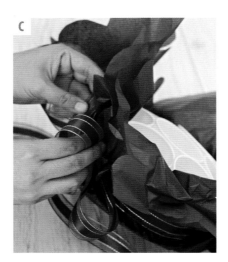

TO CREATE THIS BOUQUET...

- 7 cupcakes, muffin size
- 750g–1.1kg (1lb 10oz–2lb 7½oz) buttercream
- Paste colours: light purple (Sugarflair Grape Violet), pink (Sugarflair Pink), light green (Sugarflair Gooseberry), green (Sugarflair Spruce Green)
- 7 small plastic cups, 200ml (7fl oz) or less
- Paper plate or thick cake board, about 15–20cm (6–8in) diameter
- Tissue paper
- Cocktail sticks (toothpicks)
- Matching ribbons
- Sticky tape
- Scissors
- Artificial foliage, as accents
- Florist's card holder (optional)

Use 200–300g (7–10½oz) of plain buttercream to coat the cupcakes in a thin layer. Colour 100–150g (3½–5½oz) buttercream pink, 150–200g (5½–7oz) green, 100–200g (3½–7oz) light purple, and 200–250g (7–9oz) light green. Pipe hydrangeas (see Camellia and Hydrangea) in pale pink, and light green buttercream, roses (see Rose and Rose Bud) in pale purple and leaves (see Sunflower and Leaves) in green. Assemble the bouquet following the cup method tutorial. Decorate with tissue paper and artificial foliage, then finish with a ribbon around the base.

TIP

We highly recommend the use of sticky tape to secure the cups. Then there is no danger of staple wire getting into the cupcakes if a staple comes loose.

CUPPIE CAKE

How does the idea of a number of cupcakes being brought together to form one larger cake of your desired shape and size sound to you? Fabulous and original, isn't it? We call it a 'Cuppie Cake'! The design possibilities for this kind of cake are limitless, so have fun with it. A Cuppie Cake will never fail to raise a smile.

1 Arrange your cupcakes according to your desired shape. Make sure that they are really close together on the cake board. When you are happy with the layout, pipe a small blob of frosting on the bottom of each cake to 'glue' it to the cake board (A).

2 Pipe an even layer of buttercream on the surface of the cake and cover as a whole. Some buttercream might fall through the gaps. This is normal, and there's no need to try to fill the gaps with buttercream (B).

TIP

What is great about a Cuppie Cake is that you don't need to do any cutting of slices. With a Cuppie Cake everyone can just take a piece of cake, or shall we say cupcake, and there's no need to serve them on plates so there's no washing up either!

TO CREATE THIS CAKE...

- Covered cake board
- 7 cupcakes
- 550–950g (1lb 4oz–2lb 2oz) buttercream
- Paste colours: pink (Sugarflair Pink), dark pink (Sugarflair Claret), purple (Sugarflair Grape Violet), black (Sugarflair Black), yellow (Sugarflair Autumn Leaf), light green (Sugarflair Gooseberry) and dark green (Sugarflair Spruce Green)
- Palette knife
- Piping bags
- Scissors
- Non-toxic plants as accents (optional)

Arrange and then cover the cupcakes using 200–250g (7–9oz) of plain buttercream, following the tutorial. Colour 50–100g (1¾–3½oz) of buttercream in each of the following colours: pink, dark pink, purple, black, yellow, light green and dark green. Fill a piping bag with each colour and snip off the end to create a small hole. Pipe the floral design (see Scrolls, Lines and Zigzags, Piping Textures and Patterns).

3 Level the buttercream using a palette knife and remove the excess (C). After this, you may decorate your Cuppie Cake with whatever design you wish (D).

4 You can add some accents by inserting some ribbons or artificial or piped leaves.

PALETTE KNIFE TECHNIQUES

Using a palette knife to produce a textured surface is a stress-free technique that allows you to finish covering a cake in no time, but that is by no means the only thing you can do with a humble palette knife. Try marbling, blending and painting – you can use the knife as if you were creating an oil painting, and the results can be stunning. Master a few 'brush' strokes and away you go!

PALETTE KNIFE BRUSH STROKES

With just your palette knife you can achieve very different results by applying different strokes. There's no need to stress with sharp edges, just go with the flow and channel your inner artist. Here are the main strokes that you can use.

Vertical strokes

To achieve clean strokes, it is best to run the palette knife from the bottom of the cake upwards and not back and forth from side to side.

Horizontal/wavy strokes

Use the same basic principle as the vertical strokes, but this time, of course, move the knife horizontally. You can slightly angle your palette knife, with its tip touching the surface of the cake, then continuously turn your cake while it is on a cake turntable.

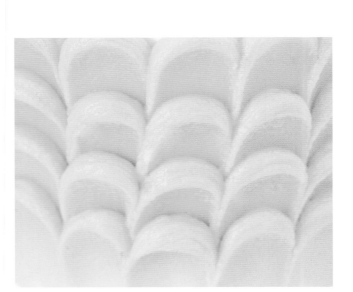

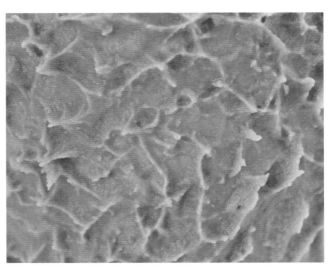

Round nozzle with palette knife

Using a simple round nozzle on a piping bag, pipe a row or column of blobs right next to each other then using the rounded tip of your palette knife, gently press down and pull towards the desired direction. Do this one row or column at a time. You can prepare colourful or gradient colours of buttercream to make this effect even more attractive.

Patting strokes

After applying your buttercream all over your cake, use the tip of your palette knife to repeatedly pat the surface all the way around while it is still sticky. This will create a unique texture.

THINNING

'Thinning', as you might guess, just means making the buttercream into a very soft and spreadable consistency by adding few drops of water. The pictures below show how thinned and unthinned consistencies behave when you spread them. The thinned buttercream is easier to spread or blend with a palette knife.

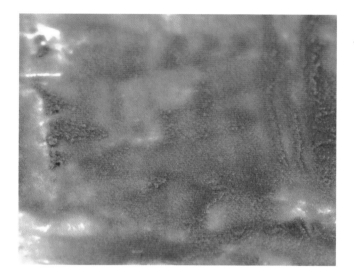

Unthinned
Rough and uneven when spread with a palette knife, unthinned buttercream is ideal for most piping and decorating. This is the consistency you will get if you follow our buttercream recipe (see Buttercream Basics).

Thinned
When thinned, your buttercream will spread in a smooth and level way, perfect for using with a palette knife to create some of the effects described on the following pages.

ABOUT PALETTE KNIVES

In this chapter we will not only use the typical palette knife that you will probably already have in your kitchen. Instead we have adapted some of the techniques used by fine artists when palette knife painting in oils, so we will also be using an artist's palette knife painting set. These can be easily purchased from most art supplies retailers. As you can see here, they have different shapes, lengths, handles and tips. Forget about the length and the way they are numbered and just look at the tips of the knives as these will be useful in determining which knife to use in a design. If you are just using a knife for spreading you can basically use any size, but if you want to use it for a more specific design, like a flower (which you will learn about in the following pages) the size of the tip becomes important. Use a small tip knife for small petals and other such details, and a big tip knife for large details. It's a simple principle!

BLENDING

This palette knife technique requires a careful choice of colours, otherwise the results can be a murky mess. Select a range of colours that complement each other and produce an over-all pleasing effect – the clashing of just two colours may ruin everything. The actual act of blending them with your knife is very simple.

1 Prepare the cake by crumb-coating it. Make sure that the tinted buttercream colours are already thinned and in individual piping bags. Cut the tip off the piping bags to create a small hole – there's no need to use a nozzle. Pipe your first colour on to the surface of the cake (A).

2 Using your palette knife, hold it about at about a 10–20 degree angle and spread the buttercream in a small circular motion (B), or with up and down strokes. Be careful not to press too hard with the knife (C).

3 Pipe your next colour but make sure you leave a small gap in between the colours. Repeat the same process to spread the buttercream and then gradually blend two colours together using the same technique (D).

4 Just keep repeating the same process until you have finished covering the cake with all the colours you have prepared (E).

TIP

It can be helpful to chill your cake first in the fridge so the surface is hard and easier to work on. The only downside is that the tinted buttercream you will apply could crust too quickly because the surface is cold. If it does, dip your palette knife in hot water when you spread the buttercream.

TO CREATE THIS CAKE...

- 20 x 15cm (8 x 6in) square cake (bottom tier), 15 x 13cm (6 x 5in) square cake (top tier)
- 2.55–3.35kg (5lb 9oz–7lb 4oz) buttercream
- Paste colours: violet (Sugarflair Grape Violet), lilac (Sugarflair Lilac), red (Sugarflair Ruby), orange (Sugarflair Tangerine), yellow (Sugarflair Autumn Leaf), light green (Sugarflair Gooseberry), dark green (Sugarflair Spruce Green)
- Palette knife
- Small petal nozzle (Wilton 104)
- Piping bags
- Scissors
- Cake stand or covered cake board

Cover, dowel and stack the cakes (see Buttercream Basics) and place on a stand or covered board. Colour and thin the buttercream in the following quantities: 250–350g (9–12oz) each of violet, lilac, red, orange, yellow, light green, dark green, and leave 250–350g (9–12oz) thinned but uncoloured. Apply and blend the colours following the tutorial and using the photograph of the finished cake as a guide. Then with the remaining plain buttercream and the small petal nozzle, pipe roses using the freezing technique so that they can be squeezed close together more easily around the base (see Rose and Rose Bud, Piping Flowers).

A
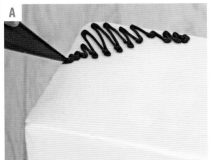

B

C

D
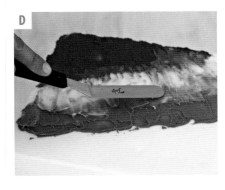

E
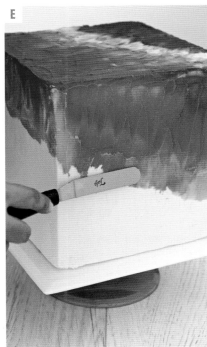

GRADIENT BLENDING AND PAINTING FLOWERS

This is a method of blending a gentle gradient of colour, and is great for creating a background on which you can 'paint' using different palette knives. These small tools will each give a different effect, and we'll show you how to use them to paint stunning flowers. What is good about palette knife painting is that you do not have to be precise with the lines and shape, it is about blending. This technique will definitely showcase the artist that you are, or will release the hidden art talent that you think you don't have.

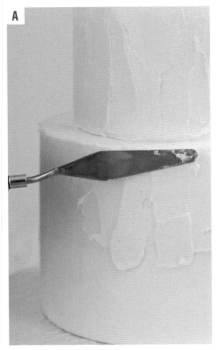

1 Select your colours and fill individual piping bags with them. Choose colours that grade from light to dark, such as the greens we have used here. Apply a textured covering of plain buttercream all over your cake (see Palette Knife Brush Strokes) (A). You will be blending the lightest of the colours with the plain buttercream before it crusts.

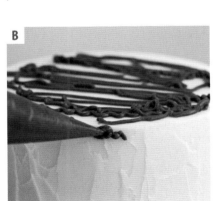

2 To create a gradient that is darkest at the top of the cake, for a sky-like effect for example, pipe the colour on to the top of the cake (B), then spread it using a palette knife (see Palette Knife Techniques, Blending). Gradually blend it into the plain buttercream (see Tip) (C).

3 To create a dark to light gradient from the base of the cake, start at the bottom edge. Using the technique described above, pipe your second colour next to the first leaving a small gap in between. Spread it, then blend the first two colours together (D). Blend the lighter colour into the plain buttercream (E).

F

4 To add more colour gradient blending effect in the background, pipe a small amount of colour on top of the white then gradually blend to the background (F).

TIP

Do not keep stroking the dark colour into the light as your dark colour will overpower your light-coloured buttercream, just gradually blend the colours.

PALETTE KNIFE FLOWERS

TIP

Look at your cake as a big canvas and decide how you will arrange your flowers. You can help to visualize the overall design by using tinted buttercream to pipe the centres of the flowers so you have a guide as to their positions.

1 For the sunflower, pipe a flower centre and guide petals, then fill them slightly using the same colour (A). Using the shorter length palette knife, position it at a 10–20 degree angle and spread the buttercream, following the shape of the petal you have piped. Stroke from the base of the petal to the tip on one side, then use the same stroke on the other side then once more up the middle (B). Avoid going back and forth so the finish is neat and always make sure to wipe your palette knife every after a stroke. Repeat to create all the petals on your first flower.

A

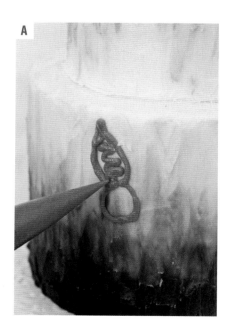

B

2 You can add a shadow effect by piping a small blob of a darker shade of tinted buttercream at the base of each of the petals then repeat the same strokes to blend this colour in (C). Pipe the centre of the flower and add dots in a lighter shade for a realistic texture (D). Repeat to create more flowers on your cake.

3 For the delphinium, outline the shape (like a big wavy teardrop) with small dots using violet tinted buttercream. Fill in with small blobs of a mix of violet, white and blue tinted buttercream (E). Using a palette knife with a fine tip, one that is almost the same size as the blob, squish the blobs down. There is no need to wipe the palette knife – the more the colours blend together, the better (F).

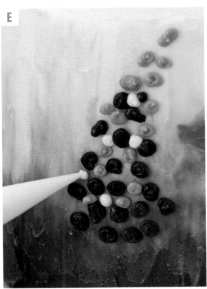

4 Finally, use dark green tinted buttercream, and a piping bag with the tip snipped off, to pipe the stems (G). There is no need to spread it as it will give another variation in texture and a three-dimensional effect.

TIP
When creating the petals at the edges of the delphinium flower spike, squish the blobs down as if you are pulling them to the centre. This will give a more defined shape and a neater result.

TO CREATE THIS CAKE...

- 25 x 15cm (10 x 6in) round cake (bottom tier), 20 x 20cm (8 x 8in) round cake (middle tier), 15 x 13cm (6 x 5in) round cake (top tier)
- 3.05–4.15kg (6lb 11oz–9lb 2oz) buttercream
- Dowel rods
- Paste colours: violet (Sugarflair Grape Violet), blue (Sugarflair Baby Blue), yellow (Sugarflair Melon), dark yellow (Sugarflair Autumn Leaf), brown (Sugarflair Dark Brown), dark brown (Sugarflair Dark Brown), mocha (Sugarflair Mocha), light green (Sugarflair Gooseberry), dark green (Sugarflair Spruce Green)
- Palette knife painting set
- Piping bags
- Scissors
- Cake stand or covered cake board

Cover, dowel and stack the cakes (see Buttercream Basics) and place on a stand or covered board. Colour the buttercream in the following quantities: 250–350g (9–12oz) each of violet, blue, yellow, dark yellow, brown, dark brown, mocha, light green and dark green. Keep 250–350g (9–12oz) for piping, and use the remaining uncoloured buttercream to cover the cake with an uneven texture (see Palette Knife Brushstrokes). Create the blended background using the two greens and most of the blue buttercream following the gradient blending tutorial. 'Paint' the flowers using the remaining colours and following the palette knife flowers tutorial.

MARBLING

Marbling is a technique where you can use as many colours as you like without having to worry that you will overwhelm your cake. In our version, you will pipe your chosen colours one after the other until there is a pattern. Afterwards, you will only have to use a simple cake comb or palette knife to blend them together which will give a more sophisticated look.

1 Decide on your overall design and mark the outline of some simple flower shapes using a cocktail stick (toothpick) (A).

2 Select as many colours as you like – in this example we used three different colours in each petal. Put all the tinted buttercream in piping bags, and use scissors to snip off the tips. Starting from the outermost petals of the flower, pipe short arches in layers of colours (B).

3 Using your cake comb or a palette knife with a large rounded tip, hold it almost flat to the cake, gently press down and drag it towards the centre of the flower. If you use a comb you will get a lovely texture and a more variegated blend (C).

4 Repeat the same process with all the petals, alternating the colours (D).

5 Depending on how big your flower is, you can also pipe two or more layers of petals, but it is important always to start at the outermost layer. Finish the flowers with a piped circle or with sprinkles.

TIP
Cake combs or zigzag cake scrapers come in different sizes but a 2.5cm (1in) wide one is useful to have. They are made of thin plastic material so you can easily cut a larger one to your desired size.

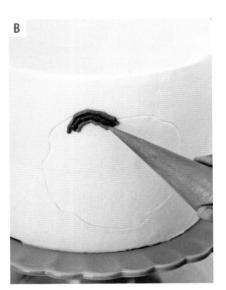

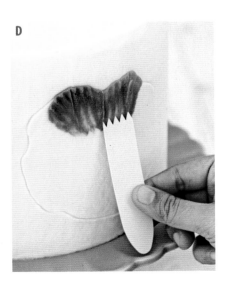

TO CREATE THIS CAKE...

- 20 x 20cm (8 x 8in) round cake
- 1.2–1.8kg (2lb 10½oz–4lb) buttercream
- Paste colours: light blue (Sugarflair Baby Blue), dark blue (Sugarflair Baby Blue), violet (Sugarflair Grape Violet), green (Sugarflair Spruce Green)
- Piping bags
- Scissors
- Cake comb or zigzag cake scraper or palette knife with large rounded tip
- White sprinkles (nonpareils)
- Cake stand or covered cake board

Crumb coat and place the cake on a stand or covered board, then give it a smooth covering using 600–800g (1lb 5oz–1lb 12oz) of uncoloured buttercream (see Covering Cakes, Buttercream Basics). Colour the remaining buttercream in the following quantities: 150–250g (5½–9oz) each of light blue, dark blue, violet and green. Create the marbled flowers following the tutorial. Apply white sprinkles to the flower centres. Pipe a thicker border at the top and bottom edges of the cake (see Scrolls, Lines and Zigzags, Piping Texture and Patterns).

TRANSFERS, STAMPING AND STENCILLING

In this chapter we look at three ways to re-create an intricate pattern on the surface of a cake. Have you seen a specific design from somewhere that you desperately want to use, *but* the details are too much to handle? Here is a solution: create a frozen buttercream transfer or FBCT! If you want a delicate pattern to cover a large area, then a stencil might be the way to achieve it, and there are hundreds of stamps to choose from to create a wide range of effects. Just delve into this chapter to find the technique that suits you.

FROZEN BUTTERCREAM TRANSFERS ON A FLAT SURFACE

Typically, when a pattern is transferred onto a cake, a border of stars or swirls is piped around the edge, making it obvious that a transferred pattern has been used. Let us show you the Queen of Hearts way! No one will even notice that you have used this technique – they will just admire the seemingly impossibly detailed pattern you have created.

1 Choose your graphic image and make sure that you re-size it so that it will fit on your cake, and create a reverse/mirror image before printing it. Next it is essential to draw a guide line around your pattern according to the exact size of your cake (A).

2 Place your pattern on a baking sheet (or any freezer-proof flat board), lay a piece of greaseproof (wax) paper on top of it and secure both with sticky tape (B).

3 Outline your pattern using different tinted buttercream if needs be. When you have done so, begin filling in colours (C). Layer in the colours as you go by finishing each one before using another. Make sure that there are no gaps in between the colours.

4 When you have finished (D), quick freeze the pattern for about 5–10 minutes until the buttercream is firm. This is important so your pattern will not move. Remove it from the freezer and, using buttercream of the same colour as the background of your cake, pipe a thin layer within and up to the guide line you drew to show the exact size of the cake (E). Spread the buttercream with a palette knife and even it out with a scraper (F). When done, freeze for about 30 minutes to an hour or until the pattern is rock hard.

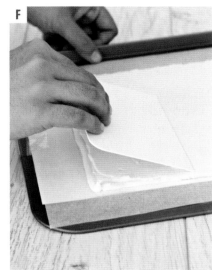

5 When the pattern is frozen, apply a thin layer of buttercream to the surface of the crumb-coated cake where you will apply the pattern, making sure it is even (G). Take the pattern out of the freezer then quickly but carefully flip it and position it on the cake, lightly pressing it down so it sticks (H). Using your palette knife, remove the excess frozen buttercream around the cake.

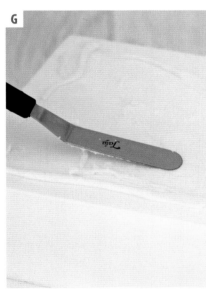

6 Using the same colour as the background, apply another layer of buttercream over all the remaining surfaces of the cake (I). Remember that it is *really important* to make this layer the same thickness as the pattern or the illusion will be spoiled. At about the same moment that you finish this, you should find that the buttercream of the pattern has become soft again. When this is so, smooth the sides and edges of the cake to a perfect finish (see Smoothing, Buttercream Basics) (J).

TO CREATE THIS CAKE...

- 20 x 10cm (8 x 4in) square cake
- 2.25–2.95kg (5lb–6lb 6oz) buttercream
- Paste colours: light pink (Sugarflair Pink), dark pink (Sugarflair Claret), dusky pink (Sugarflair Dusky Pink), foliage green (Sugarflair Foliage Green), light green (Sugarflair Gooseberry), dark green (Sugarflair Spruce Green)
- Piping bags
- Palette knife
- Scraper
- Pen
- Ruler
- Scissors
- Greaseproof (wax) paper
- Sticky tape
- Printed pattern (see Templates)
- Baking sheet or any flat board
- Small petal nozzle (Wilton 104)
- Small leaf nozzle (Wilton 352)
- Writing nozzles 1–3 (optional)
- Cake stand or covered cake board

Crumb coat (see Buttercream Basics) and place the cake on a stand or covered board. Use the template supplied to create your frozen buttercream transfer by following the tutorial. You will need to colour the buttercream in the following quantities: 200–300g (7–10½oz) each of light pink, dark pink, dusky pink, foliage green, light green and dark green. Leave 1–1.1kg (2lb 4oz–2lb 7½oz) of buttercream uncoloured to apply the transfer and cover the sides of the cake. Smooth the sides to a perfect finish (see Smoothing, Buttercream Basics). Pipe roses around the base in all the pink shades and arrange using the 'freezing' method (see Rose and Rose Bud, Piping Flowers). Add some leaves in foliage green (see Piping Flowers, Sunflowers and Leaves).

TIP
Before printing your pattern, be mindful that you need to flip or make a mirror image of the picture before you print it out. Make sure that your pattern is really frozen so your greaseproof paper will peel off easily and not stick.

FROZEN BUTTERCREAM TRANSFERS ON A CURVE

Now that you have seen how to do the flat version of a frozen buttercream transfer, you might wonder how you apply this technique to the curved side of a round cake. We have spent lots of time and loads of buttercream experimenting and perfecting a method to achieve this. Here we modestly offer you yet another brilliant innovation, brought to you exclusively by Queen of Hearts Couture Cakes!

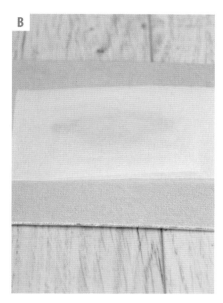

1 Choose your graphic image and make sure that you re-size accordingly and flip it to make a mirror image before printing it. Place your pattern on a baking sheet (or any flat board) with greaseproof (wax) paper on top of it. Secure the image and the greaseproof paper with sticky tape.

2 Using buttercream tinted in the colours you require, outline and fill in your pattern in layers. When you have finished, quick freeze it for about 5–10 minutes until the buttercream is firm. When the pattern is hard enough, take it out of the freezer and pipe over it with another thin layer of buttercream which is slightly bigger than the pattern (A) and smooth (B). The buttercream should be the same as the background colour of your cake.

TIP
If your pattern is big or wide you will have to divide it into several parts, freeze each and reassemble it when you apply it to the cake, repeating the process described above for each part.

3 Remove the pattern from the board and gently slide it onto the side of a round Styrofoam dummy cake. Secure it with cocktail sticks (toothpicks) or headed pins (C). Freeze the dummy with the pattern on it for about 30 minutes to an hour, or until it is rock hard. Secure it in the freezer so that it doesn't roll over.

4 When the pattern is ready, apply a thin even layer of buttercream on the surface to which you will apply it. Take the pattern out of the freezer then quickly but carefully flip it and position it on to the cake, lightly pressing it down so that the pattern sticks (D).

5 Using the same colour as the background, apply another layer of buttercream around your pattern (E) and level it using a palette knife (F). It is most important that the amount of buttercream you apply everywhere on the cake including between patterns is the same thickness as the pattern. Repeat the same process to apply any other patterns. Apply buttercream to the rest of the surface of the cake and remove any excess.

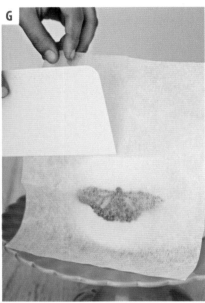

TIP
When placing a pattern over the edge of a cake, make sure the pattern is firm from freezing but not rock hard, so that it will bend to the required shape. Press it firmly on to the surface and quick freeze the whole cake again to reduce the risk of the pattern sticking to the greaseproof paper when you pull it off.

6 When cake is crusted, finish by creating a perfectly smooth surface (see Smoothing, Buttercream Basics) (G).

TIP
You can also pipe borders around your pattern once you have stuck it to your cake. If you do this, make sure you follow the shape of your pattern.

TO CREATE THIS CAKE...

- 15 x 13cm (6 x 5in) round cake
- 1.7–2.7kg (3lb 12oz–6lb) buttercream
- Paste colours: beige (Sugarflair Caramel), light blue (Sugarflair Baby Blue), dark blue (Sugarflair Navy Blue), orange (Sugarflair Tangerine), red (Sugarflair Ruby), light brown (Sugarflair Dark Brown), dark brown (Sugarflair Dark Brown), black (Sugarflair Liquorice), yellow (Sugarflair Melon)
- Piping bags
- Palette knife
- Scraper
- Pen
- Ruler
- Scissors
- Greaseproof (wax) paper
- Sticky tape
- Printed patterns (see Templates)
- Baking sheet or any flat board
- Cocktail sticks (toothpicks) or headed pins
- Styrofoam dummy cake, to match size of cake
- Writing nozzles 1–3 (optional)
- Cake stand or covered cake board

Crumb coat (see Buttercream Basics) and place the cake on a stand or covered board. Use the templates supplied to create your curved frozen buttercream transfers by following the tutorial. You will need to colour the buttercream in the following quantities: 800–900g (1lb 12oz–2lb) beige and 100–200g (3½ –7oz) each of light blue, dark blue, orange, red, light brown, dark brown, black and yellow. Leave the remaining 100–200g (3½ –7oz) of buttercream uncoloured. Apply the patterns to the cake and then cover the cake with the beige buttercream, smoothing the surface to a perfect finish (see Smoothing, Buttercream Basics). Pipe tiny flowers with the plain and yellow buttercream (see Dots, Piping Textures and Patterns).

TROUBLESHOOTING

Using frozen buttercream transfers is not difficult, but there are some pitfalls to avoid, and along the way you might encounter some problems. Do not worry – when we were experimenting we came across them too, countless times. That is why we thought we would show you some examples of what might happen, remind you *not to panic,* and offer you our solutions.

THE TRANSFER CRACKS

If your pattern cracks (A), position it on to your cake anyway, putting the broken parts as close to each other as possible (B). Where the crack is, especially if there is a gap, pipe a small amount of the same colour of buttercream over it (C) and use a small paintbrush to blend colours together (D). Then when crusted, smooth it (see Buttercream Basic chapter).

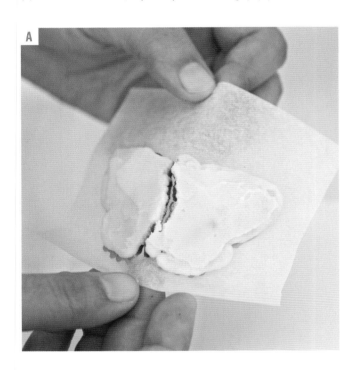

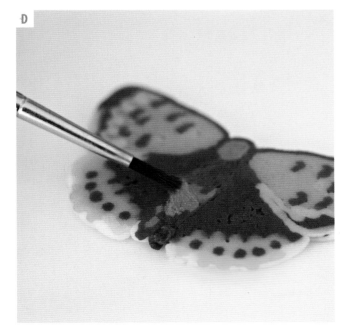

SOME DETAILS DON'T TRANSFER

Most of the time, the reason this happens is that your pattern is not sufficiently frozen and the buttercream sticks to the greaseproof (wax) paper when you try to peel it off (A). If this happens, simply pipe over the pattern again in the right colours, then blend with a brush (B). Even if you worry that you are a hopeless artist, you will be able to manage some small details. Just blending the colours with a paintbrush usually does the trick. To avoid this problem altogether, make sure that your pattern is really frozen or apply a very thin layer of vegetable fat (shortening) to the surface of the greaseproof (wax) paper before piping your design.

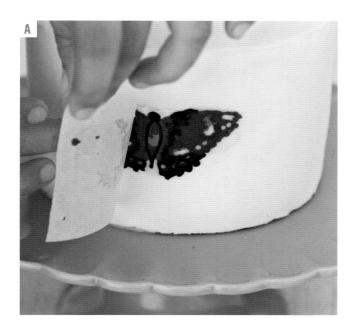

FORGETTING TO FLIP THE IMAGE

This problem is particularly bad if you are using words, letters and numbers (A). The photograph shows you what will happen if you forget to reverse the picture to get a mirror image (B). If you've already made the transfer before you spot your mistake, there is nothing you can do but remove it, or scrape it off, and re-do it again. You can print it out again or just trace your image on the greaseproof (wax) paper and do the frozen buttercream transfer on the reverse side of the paper.

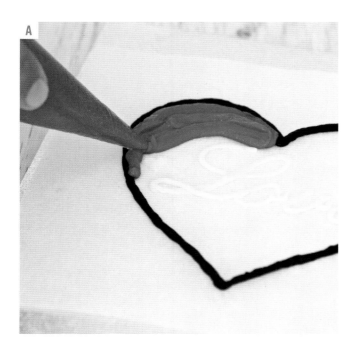

STENCILLING

Stencilling is the process of recreating a design on the surface of a cake using a ready-made stencil. This is an extremely easy technique. The grandness of your cake will rather depend on the stencil that you use. Shop around, because there are some really elegant ones that are widely available from specialist and online retailers.

1 For a 15 x 15cm (6 x 6in) stencil, put about 300–400g (10½–14oz) of tinted buttercream in a bowl and add drops of water to 'thin' it into an easily spreadable, but not runny, consistency (A). Then put it in piping bag and snip off the tip to create a small hole.

2 Cover your cake with a smooth finish (see Covering Cakes, Buttercream Basics) then put it in the fridge to chill until the surface is hard enough for you to hold the stencil against it without it sticking. This will make it easier for you to work on the cake. Position and hold the stencil on to the cake firmly then squeeze the thinned buttercream on top of the stencil (B).

3 Use a palette knife to level out the buttercream and to take off the excess (C).

4 Since the background buttercream is cold, wait until the thinned buttercream firms up a little before gently pulling the stencil away (D). Repeat the same process on the other sides of your cake.

TIP

It is best to wait for a few seconds to a minute until the design has hardened before you pull away the stencil to avoid smudging.

TO CREATE THIS CAKE...

- 15 x 15cm (6 x 6in) square cake
- 1.35–1.75kg (3lb 2oz–3lb 14oz) buttercream
- Paste colours: purple (Sugarflair Lilac), beige (Sugarflair Caramel), light green (Sugarflair Eucalyptus)
- Stencil
- Piping bags
- Palette knife
- Scissors
- Small leaf nozzle (Wilton 352)
- Small petal nozzle (Wilton 104)
- Cake stand or covered cake board

Crumb coat (see Buttercream Basics) and place the cake on a stand or covered board. Cover the cake with a smooth finish (see Covering Cakes, Buttercream Basics) using 600–800g (1lb 5oz–1lb 12oz) of purple buttercream. Colour the remaining buttercream in the following quantities: 600–700g (1lb 5oz–1lb 9oz) beige and 150–250g (5½–9oz) light green. Use the beige buttercream to create the stencil pattern on all four sides of the cake, following the tutorial. Pipe roses on the top in beige (see Rose and Rose Bud, Piping Flowers), lifting them into position with scissors, and add leaves in a mixture of beige and teal (see Sunflower and Leaves, Piping Flowers). Pipe a bottom border of shells (see Shells and Fleur-de-lis, Piping Patterns and Textures) using beige buttercream in a piping bag with the tip snipped off.

SPONGING AND STAMPING

Stamping has always been used in a wide variety of popular crafts to add a repeating pattern onto a surface. It's a technique that lends itself well to cake decorating. In our version, we take the blank canvas of a cake and, using just an ordinary sponge and different colours, we create a vibrant background that can be enhanced using small tools like cookie cutters, plungers or rubber stamps, pressed into the surface of the cake.

1 Tint buttercream in different colours, put into separate bowls and 'thin' them by adding drops of water to achieve a runny consistency (A). One of the colours should be black, or at least dark, so that it can be used for the actual stamping and will show up well against the background.

2 Cut a clean sponge into small squares and dip one in one of the bowls of thinned buttercream (B). Gently pat on smoothed surface of the cake. Use a different sponge in each colour, and make sure that before you apply the colours to the cake, you remove the excess buttercream. Repeat process until cake is covered with different colour patches, except your black or dark buttercream (C).

3 Dip your cookie cutter or flower plunger into the bowl of thinned black or dark buttercream, tap against the side of the bowl to remove any excess, and press it gently on the surface of the cake. Repeat as often as you like (D).

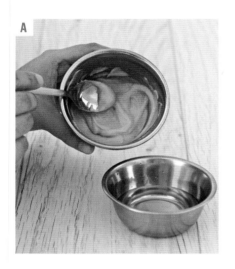

A

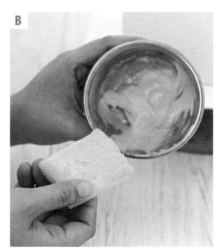

B

TIP
With this technique use white or plain buttercream to cover your cake. When applying the patches, you will only use a minimal amount of light tinted buttercream, so you need a light background for them to stand out. It is also helpful if your cake is chilled so the surface does not dent when patted.

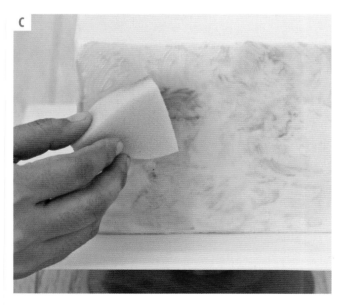

C

D

4 As a finishing touch you can add embellishments, for example you can match some coloured edible pearls to the colours of the patches and apply them by piping a small dot in the right colour and adding on a pearl using tweezers to the centre of each flower stamp (E).

TO CREATE THIS CAKE...

- 15 x 20cm (6 x 8in) square cake
- 1.5–2kg (3lb 5oz–4lb 8oz) buttercream
- Paste colours: light blue (Sugarflair Baby Blue), light green (Sugarflair Spruce Green), light yellow (Sugarflair Melon), light pink (Sugarflair Pink), black (Sugarflair Liquorice)
- Plastic bowls
- Clean sponge
- Scissors
- Small flower cookie cutter or flower plunger
- Colourful edible pearls
- Tweezers
- Piping bags
- Small petal nozzle (Wilton 104)
- Cake stand or covered cake board

Crumb coat (see Buttercream Basics) and place the cake on a stand or covered board. Cover the cake with a smooth finish (see Covering Cake, Buttercream Basics) using 600–800g (1lb 5oz–1lb 12oz) of plain buttercream. Colour the remaining buttercream in the following quantities: 150–200g (5½–7oz) each of light blue, light green, light yellow, light pink and black. Reserve a tiny quantity of each to use to stick on the edible pearls, then follow the tutorial above to colour the background and stamp the flower design. Pipe a little unthinned buttercream in the matching colour in the centre of each flower and add edible pearls. Using 150–200g (5½–7oz) unthinned light pink buttercream plus a little darker pink for the centres, pipe hydrangeas round the bottom (see Camellia and Hydrangea, Piping Flowers).

TEXTILE EFFECTS

Open your wardrobe doors and take a look at all those tops, dresses and cardigans. Notice the prints and those lovely fabric textures? In this chapter, we'll show you how to recreate these textile effects using luscious buttercream. With just a few small tools you'll be magically producing embroidery, lace and crochet like a skilled needleworker.

BRUSHED EMBROIDERY

Embroidered design, whether simple or lavish, will always add an exquisite quality. To embroider your cake, you will use a simple tool – a brush – hence, the 'brushed embroidery' technique. Flowers are particularly suited to this method, so that's what we have chosen as our example, although animals and birds and any other subject you have seen in an embroidery will work well too. Here, you will gently stroke the buttercream towards the centre of your design, leaving not only colour but also a wonderful thread-like texture on the surface of your cake.

1 If you are using an image you have found, as with buttercream pattern transfers (see Transfers, Stencilling and Stamping), make sure that you make a mirror image before you print, especially if you need to be precise with the positioning of the pattern. When the pattern is transferred, over-pipe the outline with quite a thick line of buttercream (A). If you are piping the design directly on the surface of the cake, make sure you use plenty of buttercream so you have enough to brush (B).

2 Look at your flower pattern as a whole, and imagine where the stem should be – that will be the direction where all the strokes should go. Dip your brush in a bowl of water, and wipe off the excess water with a tissue. Using your damp brush, pull the buttercream towards the centre of your flower (C). Repeat the process to the rest of the petals. If you have pulled all the buttercream, but need more to complete the flower, over-pipe the outline again slightly (D).

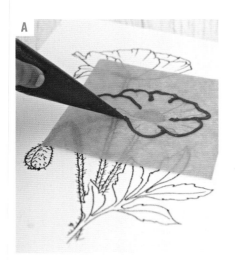

TIP
When brushing the buttercream, make sure that the paintbrush is just damp and not too wet. Some of the details are better piped, rather than brushed, to create a variation in texture.

3 Pipe the centre of the flower with dots and spikes to create a three-dimensional effect, just like real embroidery (E). There's no need to brush them but you may do so if you wish.

4 Using green tinted buttercream, pipe leaf outlines and repeat the brushed embroidery method, this time brushing towards the central vein of the leaf (F).

E

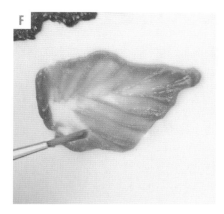
F

TO CREATE THIS CAKE...

- 25 x 15cm (10 x 6in) round cake (bottom tier), 20 x 10cm (8 x 4in) round cake (middle tier), 15 x 10cm (6 x 4in) round cake (top tier)
- 2.4–2.9kg (5lb 6oz–6lb 7oz) buttercream
- Dowel rods
- Paste colours: red (Sugarflair Ruby), black (Sugarflair Liquorice), green (Sugarflair Gooseberry)
- Small round or square tip paintbrush
- Bowl of water
- Piping bags
- Scissors
- Cake stand or covered cake board

Crumb coat then cover the top and bottom tiers using 800–900g (1lb 12oz–2lb) of uncoloured buttercream with a smooth finish (see Covering Cake, Buttercream Basics). Cover the middle tier with 400–500g (14oz–1lb 2oz) red buttercream, give it a textured finish with a palette knife (see Palette Knife Techniques). Dowel and stack the cakes (see Buttercream Basics) and place on a stand or covered board. Colour the remaining buttercream in the following quantities: 700–800g (1lb 9oz–1lb 12oz) of red, 200–300g (7–10½oz) black and 300–400g (10½–14oz) green. Refer to the photograph and follow the tutorial to paint the poppies and foliage. Pipe the centre of the flowers to add texture, using a piping bag with the tip snipped off.

LACE

Lace evokes such an elegant and timeless style, especially on a cake. There are a few lace-effect variations and each of them is equally impressive. The Irregular Lace project involves freehand piping using black-tinted buttercream on a white background to highlight the intricacy of the lace. The Fishnet Lace variation uses a piping pattern that creates connected diamonds, and we have a surprisingly easy way to achieve this effect. To make it even more interesting, we used three shades of pink-tinted buttercream to give a gradient result.

IRREGULAR LACE

1 Put black-tinted buttercream in a piping bag with or without a nozzle. You can use writing nozzle number 0 or 1. If you are not using a nozzle, cut a tiny hole at the tip of your piping bag and squeeze it onto a tissue until you get the desired thickness of the lines (A and B).

TIP
Make sure that the buttercream is lightly thinned (add few drops of water) so it becomes slightly runny and it flows smoothly.

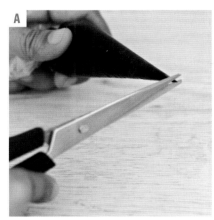

2 Place the tip of your piping bag or your nozzle very close to the surface of the cake so that the buttercream sticks to the cake and you avoid curling. Start by piping a single irregular small circle (C).

3 Continue piping small irregular circles next to each other (D). Try not to lift the bag away from the cake between circles as this will create peaks or 'spikes'. See the tip in the Fishnet Lace tutorial for dealing with these.

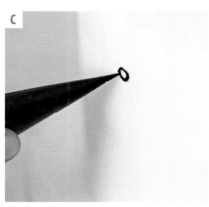
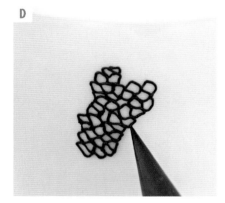

4 Continue to build up the circles making sure that all lines are connected. In this project, we started with small circles, which gradually become bigger towards the bottom of the cake (E).

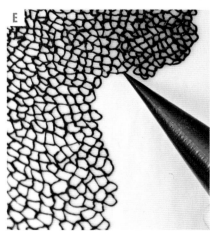

TO CREATE THIS CAKE...

- 25 x 7.5cm (10 x 3in) round cake (bottom tier), 20 x 15cm (8 x 6in) round cake (middle tier), 15 x 10cm (6 x 4in) round cake (top tier)
- 800g–1.5kg (1lb 12oz–3lb 5oz) buttercream
- Dowel rods
- Paste colours: black (Sugarflair Liquorice) green (Sugarflair Gooseberry or Spruce Green), yellow (Sugarflair Autumn Leaf), pink (Sugarflair Claret) and orange (Sugarflair Egyptian Orange)
- Writing nozzles, 0, 1 or 1.5
- Small petal nozzles (Wilton 104)
- Small leaf nozzle (Wilton 104)
- Piping bags
- Cake stand or covered cake board

Cover the cakes with a smooth finish (see Covering Cakes, Buttercream Basics), dowel and stack the cakes (see Buttercream Basics) and place on a stand or covered board. Colour 200–300g (7–10½oz) of buttercream black and add a little water to thin it. Pipe the lace as described in the tutorial, making it increasingly dense on the middle and top tiers. Colour 300–400g (10½–14oz) of buttercream in orange, pink and yellow, and use the small petal nozzle to pipe roses on the edge of the bottom and middle tiers and in the centre of the top tier, and add leaves in green using the small leaf nozzle (see Rose and Rose Bud, Piping Flowers). To finish, pipe a border at the base in black (see Scrolls, Lines and Zigzags, Piping Texture and Patterns).

FISHNET LACE

1 Prepare tinted buttercream in a couple of gradient colours and place in piping bags. You can use writing nozzle number 0 or 1. If you are not using any nozzle, just cut a tiny hole at the tip of your piping bag and squeeze it onto a tissue until you get the desired thickness of the lines (see Step 1, Irregular Lace).

2 Starting from the upper left corner of the cake and using the darkest shade of your tinted buttercream (or the lightest), pipe even sized zigzag lines horizontally (A).

3 Use the same process to pipe zigzag lines below your first row giving the impression of a diamond shape. Make sure that the points meet (B).

4 After piping a few of rows of 'diamonds', change to the next shade of buttercream and repeat the steps to build up the pattern (C).

5 To create borders or 'seams' in the fishnet effect, pipe thicker lines by applying more pressure to the piping bag as you work (D).

TO CREATE THIS CAKE...

- 15 x 13cm (6 x 5in) square cake
- 550g–1kg (1lb 4oz–2lb 3oz) buttercream
- Paste colours: pink (Sugarflair Pink), red (Sugarflair Ruby Red), green (Sugarflair Spruce Green)
- Writing nozzles: 0, 1 or 1.5
- Small petal nozzle (Wilton 103)
- Small leaf nozzle (Wilton 352)
- Piping bags
- Edible sugar balls
- Cake stand or covered cake board

Cover the cake with a smooth finish (see Covering Cakes, Buttercream Basics) and place on a stand or covered board. Colour 100–200g (3½–7oz) of buttercream in each of three shades of pink. Pipe the lace as described in the tutorial. Colour 150–250g (5½–9oz) of buttercream dark red (mix Sugarflair Pink and Ruby Red) and another 100–150g (3½–5½oz) green, and pipe the hydrangeas and leaves around the cake (see Camellia and Hydrangea, and Sunflower and Leaves, Piping Flowers). Add the edible sugar balls to the centre of each flower.

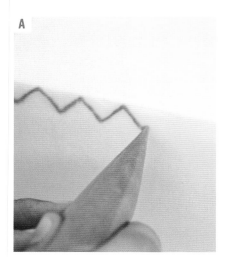

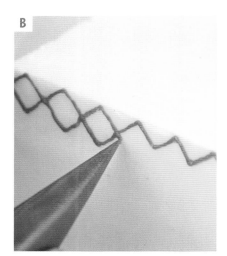

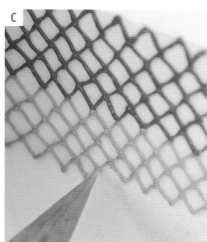

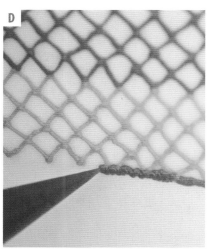

TIP

Don't lift the piping bag away from the cake as this makes peaks or 'spikes'. If you do get spikes, wait until the buttercream has crusted then press it down gently, rather than doing it while it is still fresh as it will just stick to your fingers.

CROCHET

Making a crochet gift is a labour of love — how much more so if it is an edible one? We have two variations here: the first will let you drape pretty patterns across your cake, like a shawl, using curved and straight lines. The second makes an amazing all-over texture where, just like the real thing, you make each crochet stitch one by one with a loop of piped buttercream. It's a methodical, almost soothing process that can't be hurried, but the result is a cake with charm and class.

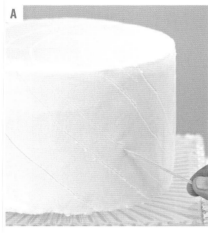

1 Using a cocktail stick (toothpick) or any pointed implement, mark patterns on the cake (A).

2 Using tinted buttercream in a piping bag, cut the tip to create a small hole. Start with the outermost line and pipe over the marked guide lines. To create the crochet effect, continuously squeeze your piping bag and as you move it along, turn your bag with a small circular motion, clockwise (B). Pipe another crochet effect line right next to the first line but do it counter-clockwise (C).

3 Repeat the process to complete the rest of the patterns on the cake (D). Create some variations by making some lines double and some just a single crochet line.

4 You may pipe a guide outline, rather than following marks, if you find it easier. Pipe a very fine outline first (E), then pipe over it using the circular crochet-making motion (F).

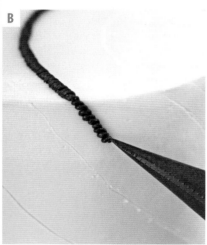

TIP
For the patterns, crochet table covers, dresses, cardigans and tops would be great inspiration.

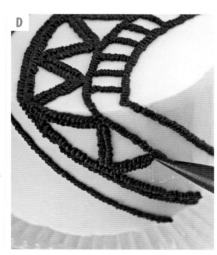

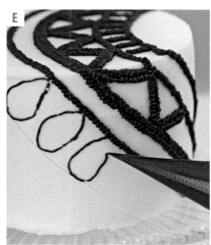

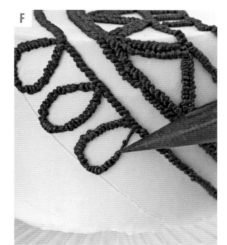

TO CREATE THIS CAKE...

- 20 x 20cm (8 x 8in) square cake (bottom tier), 15 x 10cm (6 x 4in) square cake (top tier)
- 2.35–2.75kg (5lb 4oz–6lb) buttercream
- Dowel rods
- Paste colours: green (Sugarflair Gooseberry), violet (Sugarflair Grape Violet), dark green (Sugarflair Spruce Green)
- Cocktail stick (toothpick)
- Piping bags
- Scissors
- Small petal nozzle (Wilton 104)
- Cake stand or covered cake board

Crumb coat, dowel and stack the cakes (see Buttercream Basics) and place on a stand or covered board then, referring to the photograph, mark the pattern. Cover the lower part with 800–900g (1lb 12oz–2lb) of green buttercream and the top with 800–900g (1lb 12oz–2lb) of plain buttercream, giving both a smooth finish (see Covering Cake, Buttercream Basics). Colour the remaining buttercream in the following quantities: 500–600g (1lb 2oz–1lb 5oz) violet and 250–350g (9–12oz) dark green. Refer to the photograph and follow the tutorial to pipe the crochet in violet. To give volume to the hydrangea on the corner, either pipe a big blob of buttercream or pile up a small ball of cake sponge and stick with buttercream before piping the flowers around it in dark green (see Camellia and Hydrangea, Piping Flowers). Finish with a border of crochet in dark green, piped with a bag with the tip snipped off.

LOOPED CROCHET

1 Using any straight edge tool, like a scraper or ruler, mark evenly spaced vertical lines, about 1cm (¼in) apart, all around your cake (A). This will ensure that your panels will have the same width throughout.

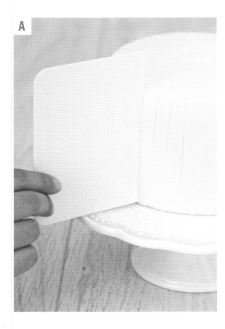

2 Choose colours then put each of your tinted buttercreams in an individual piping bag and cut a hole at the tip. Starting from the edge of the cake and working downwards, with steady pressure on your piping bag, pipe medium size counter-clockwise loops with spaces in the middle, making sure that each loop is overlapping (B).

3 Repeat the same process to create the next vertical line of clockwise crochet stitches (C). Continue until the stitches cover the whole cake. You can change the colour to add variety.

4 To finish off the top edge of the cake, pipe a crochet line as described in the first variation crochet tutorial (D).

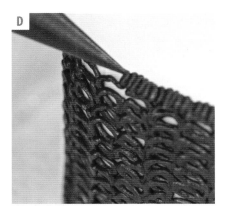

TIP
Because the whole cake is very textured do not add too many floral embellishments, as you want to focus more on the crochet design rather than the flowers.

TO CREATE THIS CAKE...

- 20 x 10cm (8 x 4in) round cake (bottom tier), 15 x 18cm (6 x 7in) round cake (middle tier), 10 x 10cm (4 x 4in) round cake (top tier)
- 2.8–3.5kg (6lb 4oz–7lb 11oz) buttercream
- Dowel rods
- Paste colours: biege (Sugarflair Caramel), green (Sugarflair Gooseberry), brown (Sugarflair Dark Brown), burgundy (Sugarflair Burgundy), grey (Sugarflair Liquorice), white (Sugarflair Super White), dark yellow (Sugarflair Autumn Leaf)
- Scraper or ruler
- Piping bags
- Scissors
- Leaf nozzle (Wilton 352)
- Cake stand or covered cake board

Crumb coat, dowel and stack the cakes (see Buttercream Basics) and place on a stand or covered board. Cover and smooth the cakes using 900g–1kg (2lb–2lb 4oz) of plain buttercream (see Covering Cake, Buttercream Basics). Colour the remaining buttercream in the following quantities: 200–300g (7–10½oz) beige, 100–200g (3½–7oz) each of green and brown, 600–700g (1lb 5oz–1lb 9oz) burgundy, 150–200g (5½–7oz) grey, 50–100g (1¾–3½oz) white and 700–800g (1lb 9oz–1lb 12oz) dark yellow. Refer to the photograph and follow the tutorial to pipe the crochet in dark yellow, burgundy, grey and white. Finish the top edge of each cake and the bottom with a row of crochet following the first variation tutorial. Pipe a sunflower at the base of the top tier with beige buttercream (see Sunflower and Leaves, Piping Flowers), and complete its centre with dots of green and brown.

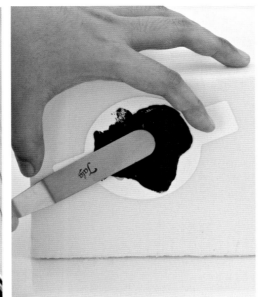

WRITING

Think of a personalized cake given your own special touch with a heartfelt written message – you'd love to be able to do it, but you're worried that you'll ruin your otherwise beautifully decorated cake. Of all the skills to master, piped writing seems to be the most daunting. But never fear! We have lots of suggestions to help. You can learn to pipe the words freestyle or with a little help from some small tools – ideal for those whose handwriting suffers from artistic shortcomings (or is nearly illegible).

DIRECT PIPING

This approach is for those who scribble confidently and write legibly. With this technique, you will write the words by directly piping the buttercream on to the cake. Given the right grip and proper pressure on the piping bag, you will be able to achieve perfect handwriting.

EFFECTS OF NOZZLES

In the column below we used five different kinds of nozzles to write one word – LOVE – but this is just a fraction of the range of nozzles that you can use. You can see that on changing the nozzle, the overall effect of the word will change, giving different character to the cake.

DIFFERENT WRITING STYLES

Below we have also shown just a few of the many styles of writing that you might want to use. Again, the style you choose will have an effect on the overall impression the cake gives – from zany to romantic. All the examples in the column below were piped with a writing nozzle.

Writing nozzle

Simple round nozzle

Small star nozzle

Chrysanthemum nozzle

Basketweave nozzle

- Buttercream
- Piping bags
- Scissors
- Writing nozzle 0-3 (optional)

TIP
Another trick for better freehand writing that we use is to measure the width of the space where we are going to write and draft the words on paper first. Then we can check that the words will fit into that space before we pipe on the cake.

You can either use a writing nozzle or just cut a small hole at the tip of your piping bag to write your words. When you write, make sure that the tip of your nozzle or your piping bag lightly touches the surface of your cake so that the buttercream does not curl. Ideally, hold your piping bag straight and make sure you squeeze it with even pressure, from the beginning of a word to the end, so the thickness will be the same throughout. It is also helpful to rest your wrist very gently on the corner of the cake or use your other hand to support your dominant hand while writing, so it is not too shaky. It is a good idea to use a cocktail stick (toothpick) to mark the surface of the cake with a couple of dots to show yourself where to start and finish, or use the pattern transfer technique (see Pattern Transfer).

PAINTING

This technique can be both easy and tricky at the same time. Easy because the writing tool is a paintbrush, which means you will have enough tolerance to outline, paint and then go back over to improve your handwriting. But it can be tricky because you will be painting straight onto a very delicate buttercream surface. Nonetheless, result will be more artistic compared to the other forms of writing.

YOU WILL NEED...

- Food colouring gel/paste or lustre dust of your choice
- Small round tip paintbrush
- Paint palette
- Water, rejuvenating alcohol, vodka or lemon juice

TIP
We suggest using food colouring paste or gel diluted with water, rather than vodka or lemon juice so that it doesn't alter the taste of the buttercream. Paste or gel will give a deeper colour than edible lustre dust.

1 It is best to draft your message on a piece of paper the same size as your cake to make sure that your words will fit and you are happy with the position. It is also helpful to look at different fonts for inspiration and variation. Use food colouring paste/gel and slightly dilute it with either water, rejuvenating alcohol, vodka or lemon juice (A). Note that if you use edible lustre dusts, you may use any of these except water. It is best to use a small round tip brush to paint your patterns or letters.

2 Dip your paintbrush in the food colouring and wipe off the excess. Carefully write your message directly on to the surface of the cake. On the first go, the letters will be very light and just like a mere outline. At this stage you can make slight changes to your pattern. When you are happy with it, paint over it again until it is the required colour (B).

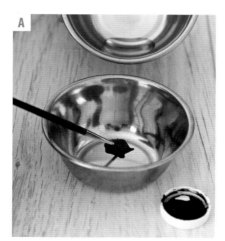

PATTERN TRANSFER

Does your handwriting look unidentifiable sometimes, or even most of the time, but you want very much to write a personal message on your cake? Well, handwriting will not be an issue if you use a pattern. You will just need to type your own words in a document on your computer, carefully choose your font style and there you go – you have a clearly defined printed pattern.

YOU WILL NEED...

- Buttercream
- Piping bags
- Scissors
- Printed pattern
- Greaseproof (wax) paper/clear acetate or any transparent material

1 Choose your font from your computer and type your message in a document file. Before printing it out, make sure you adjust the size to exactly how you want it, so that it will fit on your cake, and flip it to make a mirror image before you print it (A).

2 Cut the excess paper from around your pattern. Using clear acetate, greaseproof (wax) paper or any clean transparent material to put on top of the pattern, trace your letters by piping over them using a bag with a very small hole cut in the tip (B).

3 When done, take the tracing paper and position it on to the cake, lightly press it down (C) and peel off (D). Re-trace or over-pipe again to finish.

TIP

It seems obvious, but before you print out your pattern, don't forget to check your spelling. It takes just a second, especially if you use a spellchecker, but will save you a lot of time if you spot a mistake.

EMBOSSING OR STENCILLING

Of all the writing techniques, embossing or stencilling will give you the sharpest and most intricate results. Here, you will be able to achieve the exact shape, size and overall style of your pattern because you will use embossers or stencils. Using this tool also reduces the time you need to finish you cake – you'll have your couture cake ready in no time!

YOU WILL NEED...

- Buttercream (slightly thinned)
- Piping bags
- Scissors
- Embossers/stencils
- Palette knife
- Writing nozzle 0-3 (optional)

1 Make sure that the buttercream is slightly thinned (see Palette Knife Brushstrokes, Palette Knife Techniques). If using an embosser, you just have to press the tool slightly onto the surface of the cake, then over-pipe with buttercream.

2 If using a stencil, position the stencil on to the cake and apply the slightly thinned buttercream from a piping bag (A). Lightly spread the buttercream with a palette knife (B) then peel off the stencil (C).

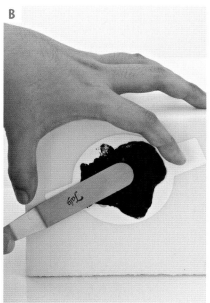

TIP
Stencilling works best if you chill your cake in the fridge for a short while. This will stop the stencil sticking to the surface when you peel it off and solidifies the pattern which prevents it smudging.

USING WRITING CREATIVELY

There are times when spoken words are not enough, and you would rather say it in style and surprise somebody special by putting your message on a cake. With buttercream you can express anything you want to say – how cool, and at the same time sweet, is that? The following tutorial combines all the writing techniques we have described in this chapter and shows you how to put them together to make the stunning graffiti cake pictured opposite. All the words on the cake mean 'love'.

1 Using your ruler or scraper, mark a bottom border. Using various colours of tinted buttercream, pipe different colour squares (see Crochet, Textile Effects).

TIP

If you are going to use stencilling and embossing always do these two techniques first, before you do any other piping, because you need to be certain that you have sufficient space to fit the stencils and patterns on the cake.

2 Start with the stencilling technique (see Stencilling and Embossing) as you need ample space to do this (A). Make sure to use thinned buttercream.

A

3 Next use some embossers (see Stencilling and Embossing) to make an impression and then pipe over it.

4 Lastly, you can write other words or patterns using freehand piping or painting (see Direct Piping, Pattern Transfer and Painting) as you can easily adjust the size of your lettering to fit into the spaces that are left. You can also fill empty spaces by piping simple shapes.

TO CREATE THIS CAKE...

- 20 x 25cm (8 x 10in) square cake (bottom tier), 15 x 13cm (6 x 5in) square cake (top tier)
- 2.3–3kg (5lb 2oz–6lb 8oz) buttercream
- Dowel rods
- Paste colours: red (Sugarflair Ruby), pink (Sugarflair Pink), dusky pink (Sugarflair Dusky Pink), burgundy (Sugarflair Burgundy), black (Sugarflair Liquorice)
- Scraper or ruler
- Piping bags
- Scissors
- Embossers and stencils
- Palette knife
- Small round tip paintbrush
- Black food colouring gel/paste
- Water, rejuvenating alcohol, vodka or lemon juice
- Paint palette
- Writing nozzle 0-3 (optional)
- Cake stand or covered cake board

Crumb coat, dowel and stack the cakes (see Buttercream Basics) and place on a stand or covered board. Cover and smooth the cakes using 900g–1kg (2lb–2lb 4oz) of plain buttercream (see Covering Cakes, Buttercream Basics). Colour the remaining buttercream in the following quantities: 200–300g (7–10½oz) each of red, pink, dusky pink and burgundy, 300–400g (10½–14oz) of black and another 300–400g (10½–14oz) of black again, but this time slightly thinned. Refer to the photograph and pipe the crochet borders in red, pink, blue and dusky pink and burgundy (see Crochet, Textile Effects). Add the words and patterns following the tutorial, using the black and thinned black buttercream and the black food colouring gel/paste.

BEYOND BUTTERCREAM

Just when you thought that sweets and candies were only for kids… In this chapter we will prove to you just how pretty those colourful treats are, especially when arranged cleverly on your cake. Everyday food, such as fruit loop cereal or a bag of humbugs can have a transforming effect. They create perfect accents, making them a double treat!

EMBELLISHMENT CHOICES

Colourful candies, chocolates, and so many other edible sweeties would make lovely adornments to your cake. Choose sweets that either complement or make a good contrast to the colour of your tinted buttercream. Round shaped sweets can be lovely when put in the middle of a flower, will make great borders, and can be arranged to create shapes or words. Just remember that some things, like cookies and marshmallows, if left exposed for a few days will become stale or dry. Here is a selection of our favourite embellishments. Whatever you choose make sure to pipe a blob of buttercream to stick them to your cake.

Multi-coloured edible sugar balls

Flying saucer sherbets

Gold edible sugar balls

Oreos

Marshmallows

Gummy laces

Printed rice paper

Liquorice

Fruit Loops (cereal)

Pink edible
sugar balls

Chocolate buttons

Blue edible sugar balls

White
chocolate
buttons

Sprinkles (nonpareils/
hundreds and thousands)

Sweets (candies)

RICE PAPER

This one is something that can be done in a flash! As we like to say, 'imagination is your only limitation'. All you have to do is get the perfect picture in your head, and go out and find it. You may take photos of real life, or simply search the web. Be aware of copyright issues if you want to use a photograph that was taken by someone else. Send off your image to a specialist supplier to be printed on an edible material like rice paper or icing sheet and stick it on to the cake. Voila!

1 Once you have had your image printed on to either rice paper or hardened icing sheet, decide on its position on your cake, trim it to size (A) and peel off any backing paper (B).

A

RICE PAPER VERSUS ICING SHEET

Rice paper is basically like a sheet of paper, only edible, but an icing sheet (below) is slightly thicker, heavier and very flexible. It will not remain stiff without backing support, so it is best to apply icing sheet flat onto the cake. On rice paper, colours are not as bright and rich as when printed on an icing sheet, though you can boost the colours by painting brighter edible colours or using edible colour pens on a rice paper image. If you do, make sure you do not use too much liquid as it will dissolve and wrinkle the paper. For the icing sheet, have your image printed, cut around it and leave it uncovered. It will eventually harden and becomes easier to stick onto the cake. Be very careful though as it tends to become very brittle.

2 Pipe a small amount of buttercream on to the surface of the cake to act as 'glue', and spread evenly with a palette knife (C) before sticking on the pattern (D).

TIP
To prevent colours from bleeding you can spray the rice paper or icing sheet pattern with an edible glaze.

B

C

D

3 To make the butterfly look more interesting, give it a slight fold in the middle before sticking it onto the cake (E). Don't try this with an icing sheet – it only works with rice paper.

4 Optionally, you may add some piped details to give variations in texture.

TO CREATE THIS CAKE...

- 20 x 10cm (8 x 4in) round cake (bottom tier), 15 x 10cm (6 x 4in) round cake (top tier)
- Dowel rods
- 1.4–1.8kg (3lb 1½oz–4lb) buttercream
- Paste colours: violet (Sugarflair Grape Violet), yellow-green (Sugarflair Bitter Melon), yellow (Sugarflair Melon)
- Piping bags
- Scissors
- Palette knife
- Cake scraper
- Pattern printed on rice paper or icing sheet
- Cake stand or covered cake board

Crumb coat, dowel and stack the cakes (see Buttercream Basics) and place on a stand or covered board. Colour the buttercream in the following quantities: 300–400g (10½–14oz) each of violet, yellow-green and yellow, leaving 500–600g (1lb 2oz–1lb 5oz) plain. To cover the cake, apply the tinted buttercream in layers and spread using a palette knife to give a blended background for the cake (see Blending, Palette Knife Techniques), before you take off the excess using a cake scraper. Give the cake a smooth finish (see Smoothing, Buttercream Basics). Scan the templates supplied to create rice paper or icing sheet patterns, and apply them to the cakes following the tutorial.

SPRINKLES

Known variously as sprinkles or nonpareils or hundreds and thousands, sprinkles are basically coloured beads made of sugar. On ordinary cakes, you might just cover the whole cake with these tiny balls but then, as you know, we don't want an ordinary cake, we want a couture cake! So what we have done here is to create a cut-out pattern to mask an area of the cake. The whole of the cake is then covered with sprinkles and when the mask is removed it leaves the pattern. These tiny balls are not just for topping your cupcakes, they can be used in a fabulous design.

1 After covering your cake with a smooth finish, put it in the fridge to chill and prepare your pattern. You can either print a pattern out then copy on to the greaseproof (wax) paper and cut or draw it freehand (A).

2 Remove your cake from the fridge and position your cut-out pattern on the cake surface as a mask (B). The pattern should stick straight onto the cake as it is covered with buttercream, but you can apply a very thin layer of butter or vegetable fat (shortening) to the greaseproof paper.

3 Prepare your sprinkles (nonpareils) by pouring a mix of red and white onto a large shallow tray (C). With pieces of greaseproof paper between your hands and the cake to protect it, and if the cake is small, lift it and place it into the tray of sprinkles with the front side down (D). Gently but firmly press it down so that the sprinkles adhere to the buttercream. Repeat the same process on all of the sides of the cake.

4 Remove the excess sprinkles with a cocktail stick (toothpick) (E) then carefully remove the paper mask.

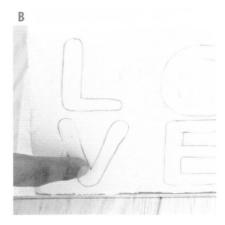

TIP
If you use a small cake it is easy just to turn and roll it in the bed of sprinkles. If your cake is relatively big do not attempt this, just use a spoon to scoop the sprinkles and gently press them all around the cake.

TO CREATE THIS CAKE...

- 15 x 13cm (6 x 5in) square cake (bottom tier), 10 x 10cm (4 x 4in) square cake (top tier)
- Dowel rods
- 1.3–1.6kg (3lb–3lb 8oz) buttercream
- Paste colours: sky blue (Sugarflair Baby Blue), beige (Sugarflair Caramel)
- Greaseproof (wax) paper
- Pen
- Scissors
- Red and white sprinkles (nonpareils)
- Large shallow tray
- Piping bags
- Cocktail stick (toothpick)
- Small petal nozzle (Wilton 104)
- Cake stand or covered cake board

Crumb coat the cakes (see Buttercream Basics) then cover the top tier with 500–600g (1lb 2oz–1lb 5oz) of sky blue buttercream and the bottom tier with 600–700g (1lb 5oz–1lb 9oz) of plain, giving both a smooth finish (see Covering Cake, Buttercream Basics). Place the bottom tier cake in the fridge to chill. Follow the tutorial to create the sprinkles (nonpareils) pattern on the bottom tier. Dowel and stack the cakes (see Buttercream Basics) and place on a stand or covered board. Colour 200–300g (7–10½oz) buttercream beige, pipe a rose (see Rose and Rosebud, Piping Flowers) and position it on the top of the bottom tier.

CANDIES

Here's another way to make cake decorating incredibly easy – just don't tell anyone how simple it is! Gather together some colour-matching sweeties that will complement the background colour of your cake. Just position these to create a pattern, and enhance it with simple piped flowers or even swirls to further lift the look.

1 Remove any sweet (candy) wrappers. Pipe a blob of colour-matching buttercream at the back of each sweet (A). Arrange and stick them all around the bottom of the cake.

2 Pipe a border of small shells (see Shells and Fleur-de-lis, Piping Textures and Patterns) using a small star nozzle (Wilton 16) above the row of sweets to make it look more artistic and to neaten the effect (B).

3 Cut the liquorice into small circles about 1cm (½in) thick using scissors (C). Make sure they are even in thickness.

4 Arrange and push the liquorice circles into the buttercream surface of the cake with even spaces (D). There is no need to pipe buttercream underneath each piece of liquorice. Repeat the process until the circles are distributed evenly over the whole cake.

TO CREATE THIS CAKE...

- 15 x 30cm (6 x 8in) round cake
- 1.9–2.4kg (4lb 3oz–5lb 6oz) buttercream
- Paste colours: black (Sugarflair Liquorice), green (Sugarflair Spruce Green), light green (Sugarflair Gooseberry), pale violet (Sugarflair Grape Violet)
- Black liquorice sweets (candies)
- Black and white striped mints (humbugs)
- Scissors
- Piping bags
- Small star nozzle (Wilton 16)
- Small petal nozzle (Wilton 103)
- Small leaf nozzle (Wilton 352)
- Cake stand or covered cake board

Crumb coat (see Buttercream Basics) then cover the cake with 800–900g (1lb 12oz–2lb) of plain buttercream. Give it a smooth finish (see Covering Cake, Buttercream Basics) and place on a stand or covered board. Colour the remaining buttercream in the following quantities: 200–300g (7–10½oz) each of green, light green and pale violet, and 500–600g (1lb 2oz–1lb 5oz) black. Apply the sweets and piped shell border by following the tutorial and using the photograph as a guide. Pipe two-tone Hydrangeas in light green and pale violet (see Camellia and Hydrangea, Piping Flowers) over the top and cascading down the sides of the cake. Add some leaves in green (see Sunflower and Leaves, Piping Flowers).

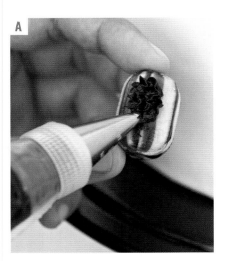

TIP
Choose matching colour sweets that will complement the colour theme for your cake – candies, marshmallows, chocolate drops or anything else you fancy.

CEREALS

You will be surprised how a handful of humble breakfast cereal loops can make a really cute decorative pattern. Not to mention the almost effortless job of popping them onto your cake. An added benefit is the amazing contrast in textures produced by the crunchiness of the cereal, the lusciousness of the buttercream and the moist cake sponge – every bite is exciting!

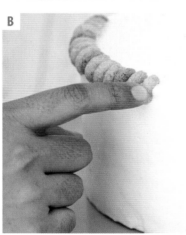

1 Using a small kitchen knife, carefully cut the cereal loops in half (A).

2 Starting from the edge at the top of the cake, arrange and stick the cereal loops next to each other, alternating the colours, all around the cake (B). Make sure that there are no gaps in between.

3 Repeat the same process all over the sides of the cake, until they are completely covered (C).

4 To cover the top of the cake, use whole cereal loops and press them lightly onto the surface of the cake, making sure there are no gaps (D).

> **TIP**
> The cake should be covered with a good amount of buttercream, a little over 0.5cm (¼in), so that the loops can be securely embedded into the cake surface.

TO CREATE THIS CAKE...

- 20 x 10cm (8 x 4in) round cake (bottom tier), 15 x 10cm (6 x 4in) round cake (top tier)
- 1.9–2.3kg (4lb 3oz–5lb 3oz) buttercream
- Dowel rods
- Paste colours: violet (Sugarflair Grape Violet), green (Sugarflair Gooseberry), yellow (Sugarflair Melon)
- Breakfast cereal, we have used Fruit Loops here
- Small kitchen knife
- Piping bags
- Scissors
- Small petal nozzle (Wilton 104)
- Small leaf nozzle (Wilton 352)
- Cake stand or covered cake board

Crumb coat, dowel and stack the cakes (see Buttercream Basics) and place on a stand or covered board. Cover both tiers with 800–900g (1lb 12oz–2lb) of plain buttercream. Give the top tier a smooth finish (see Covering Cake, Buttercream Basics) and pipe ruffles on the bottom tier using 800–900g (1lb 12oz–2lb) of buttercream tinted yellow (see Up and Down Ruffles, Piping Textures and Patterns). Colour the remaining buttercream in the following quantities: 200–300g (7–10½oz) of violet and 100–200g (3½–7oz) of green. Apply the cereal loops by following the tutorial and using the photograph as a guide. To finish the cake, pipe a violet buttercream flower with green leaves (see Sunflower and Leaves, Piping Flowers) and give it a cereal loop centre.

TEMPLATES

The templates shown here can be enlarged to your desired size by scanning or photocopying.

Butterflies

© www.scorpydesign.com

http://vector4free.com/
vector/butterfly-vector/

**Elegance Illustration
with Pink Flowers**

© www.flowervector.com

http://www.flowervector.com/
elegance-illustration-with-
pink-flowers-1034.html

Pansies
Adapted from an original
design © Dominica Alcátara

SUPPLIERS

UK SUPPLIERS

Lindy's Cakes Ltd.
Unit 2, Station Approach, Wendover,
Buckinghamshire, HP22 6BN
+44(0)1296 622 418
www.lindyscakes.co.uk
Online shop for cookie cutters and stencils

Edible Creators Ltd.
191 Station Road, Rainham, KENT ME8 7SQ
+44 (0)1634 235407 / 075813 95801
www.ediblecreatorsltd.com
Supplier of impression mats and texture sheets

Decobake Ltd.
Unit 1, Clane Business Park, Clane,
Co. Kildare, Ireland
+35 (045) 893 890
www.decobake.com
Big selection of cake decorating supplies

Cake Stuff Ltd.
Milton Industrial Estate
Lesmahagow
Scotland ML11 0JN
+44 (0)1555 890 111
www.cake-stuff.com
Supplier of cake decorating materials

The Cake Decorating Company
Unit 2b Triumph Road, Nottingham NG7 2GA
+44 (0)115 969 9800
www.thecakedecoratingcompany.co.uk
Range of cake decorating materials and edible printing

DinkyDoodle Designs
2b Triumph Road, Nottingham, NG7 2GA
+44 (0)115 969 9803
www.dinkydoodledesigns.co.uk
Supplier of airbrush machines and colours

Knightsbridge PME Ltd.
Riverwalk Business Park, Riverwalk Rd, Enfield EN3 7QN
+44 (0)20 3234 0049
www.knightsbridgepme.co.uk

US SUPPLIERS

The Cake World
184 Broadway #15 (Route 1N) -
Saugus, MA 01906 – 781-558-5508
+1 781-558-5508
www.thecakeworld.net
Supplier of cake decorating materials

ABC Cake Decorating Supplies/Cake Art
2853 E Indian School Rd
Phoenix, AZ. 85016
+1 602-224-9796
www.cakearts.com
Supplier of cake decorating materials and edible printing

ACKNOWLEDGMENTS

All our ideas and passion for cake decorating would not have been translated into these lovely pages if it weren't for our publisher, F&W Media. So for this, we would like to thank each and every one of you: Ame Verso, Jane Trollope, Emma Gardner, Victoria Marks, James Brooks and the rest of the team. To our amazing photographers, Sian Irvine and Nick Hayes, thank you so much for being so patient and making sure that each shot was perfect.

Two years ago, we were just selling cupcakes in school fairs but Cake International show organizers gave us the chance to be part of the real world of cakes. They were the first who invested trust in us and they have played a major role in allowing us to showcase our talents to the world. To Clare Fisher, Ben Fidler, David Bennett, Vicki Vinton, and the rest of the team, thank you ever so much. To all the judges we have met in different cake competitions, you have been our best critics and you have pushed us to improve our craft in so many ways.

To our dearest friend and member of Team QoHCC, Maureen Tungol, thank you much for always helping us and only expecting cupcakes and a nice dinner in return. To all our enthusiastic friends and followers all over the world, this page would not be enough to write all your names, but you know who you are and we thank each and every one of you for your continuous support.

Above all, we would like to offer our utmost gratitude to our ever supportive families back in the Philippines. Thank you for being the best fan group ever, we hope that we have made you proud. We dedicate this book to all of you.

ABOUT THE AUTHORS

Valeri Valeriano and Christina Ong left the Philippines in 2008 to work in the UK in the medical field. After the 'sweet accident' of learning how to make cupcake bouquets in 2011, they launched their business Queen of Hearts Couture Cakes and have since won several top awards in various prestigious cake competitions.

Now renowned globally for their edible works of art, using nothing else but buttercream as their decorating medium, Valeri and Christina have been featured in numerous well-known magazines and on local and international news. They have appeared on television, and showcased their masterpieces and demonstrated their craft in major cake shows in the UK and abroad. They hold masterclasses in the UK, Europe, Asia and the US and have also held a couple of masterclasses at the famous Victoria & Albert Museum, London.

Valeri and Christina take immense pride in their mastery of buttercream art and this makes Queen of Hearts Couture Cakes exclusive. They have modernized what is commonly known as the age-old art of buttercream, and this is reflected in their creations. Their cake designs are elegant, original and eminently contemporary.

Find out more at
www.queenofheartscouturecakes.com and
www.facebook.com/QueenofHeartsCupcakesAndMore

PHOTO INDEX

86 FLOWERS, PIPING ON CAKE

82 FLOWERS, ROSE & ROSE BUD

62 FLOWERS, SUNFLOWER & LEAVES

111 FROZEN BUTTERCRAM TRANSFERS, CURVED

108 FROZEN BUTTERCREAM TRANSFERS, FLAT

126 LACE, FISHNET

124 LACE, IRREGULAR

54 LEAF TEXTURE

58 LINES & ZIGZAGS

104 MARBLING

38 RUFFLES, BACK & FORTH

42 RUFFLES, SQUIGGLY

40 RUFFLES, UP & DOWN TWO-TONE

48 SCROLLS, E- & C-

56 SHELLS & FLEUR-DE-LIS

118 SPONGING & STAMPING

50 STAR FILL

116 STENCILLING

138 WRITING

INDEX

A DAVID & CHARLES BOOK
© F&W Media International, Ltd 2014

David & Charles is an imprint of F&W Media International, Ltd
Brunel House, Forde Close, Newton Abbot, TQ12 4PU, UK

F&W Media International, Ltd is a subsidiary of F+W Media, Inc
10151 Carver Road, Suite #200, Blue Ash, OH 45242, USA

Text and Designs © Valeri Valeriano and Christina Ong 2014
Layout and Photography © F&W Media International, Ltd 2014, except those listed on p.152–3

First published in the UK and USA in 2014

Valeri Valeriano and Christina Ong have asserted their rights to be identified as authors
of this work in accordance with the Copyright, Designs and Patents Act, 1988.

A catalogue record for this book is available from the British Library.

ISBN-13: 978-1-4463-0397-9 paperback
ISBN-10: 1-4463-0397-7 paperback

ISBN-13: 978-1-4463-0398-6 hardback
ISBN-10: 1-4463-0398-5 hardback

Printed in Italy by G. Canale & C. S.p.A. for:
F&W Media International, Ltd
Brunel House, Forde Close, Newton Abbot, TQ12 4PU, UK

10 9 8 7 6 5 4 3 2 1

Acquisitions Editor: Ame Verso
Desk Editor: Emma Gardner
Project Editor: Jane Trollope
Senior Designer: Victoria Marks
Photographers: Sian Irvine and Nicholas Hayes
Senior Production Controller: Kelly Smith

F+W Media publishes high quality books on a wide range of subjects.
For more great book ideas visit: **www.stitchcraftcreate.co.uk**